Beyond The Visible Spectrum

Stories from a personal quest to explore the spiritual perspectives of the world

D1264125

By **Allan Ward**

Cover illustration: Jo Ann Donaldson

Award Press
6609 Sherry Drive
Little Rock, Arkansas 72204
alward@ualr.edu

Printed in the United States of America

Introduction

At twelve, I determined to explore all religions, denominations, sects, cults, and worldviews possible. The impulse was fueled by the awareness of hundreds, of thousands of religions, and by the compelling questions, Where do they lead? Where have they led those who have followed them?

The private quest began with local groups and spread with travels to all of the continental states. It evolved into a search for the human understanding of the concepts of enlightenment and spirituality. In time, I conversed with dwellers of the Amazon, with the Hindus of Katmandu, the Buddhists of Bangkok, with Coptics and Moslems in the shadow of the Egyptian pyramids, with the Orthodox in sight of the Greek Parthenon, with dwellers in *evil-free* circular Zulu huts, in lofts and basements and temples where followers praised multitudes of self-proclaimed new messengers attempting to replace earlier religions, with *museum Christians* in Australia, and with New Age singers in a hand-holding circle in the ancient plaza of Machu Picchu in the Andes.

As the search spread over six continents, my focus centered on individuals telling the stories of their journeys among the alleys of cities, the rain-forest trails, and among the star-paths of mythologies, and the novas of epiphanies. When I asked people across the earth for the tales of their pathways, some inquired of my journey. To questions of *how did it start*, and *what happened next,* and *what is the synthesis,* my responses were these stories of the voyage of discovery.

We begin with this poem that gestures toward the mysteries that wait to be discovered together, as we journey upward through the caverns of our limited awareness, on our mutual adventure.

Beyond the Visible Spectrum

echoes of their chants within caverns
tempting with shadows of something more
just beyond the torchlight

intuitively seeking on a quest worded with whispers
and songs of tentative notes
rhythms rapturous and raw
where concluding chords
evolve into the prelude of the melody to come

feelings amid the stalactites
the underworld pools and rapids
sensations searing soothing
hanging in the air
more queries than responses
unseen bat wings rustling *why*
along the concave walls

enough distantly reverberate
wolvine howls in the labyrinth
through some sinkhole
from another level in the maze
never enough
they say without words
perceiving possibilities further on
just beyond
possibilities bubbling in pits emitting fumes
of unnamed scents of undiscovered essences
attar of living

tunnels lead to paradigms
through streaks of smoldering ebony
and the reflections from the eyes
of phantom dragons

within the unmeasured realm
of subterranean chambers
an alien-palated rainbow glows
misty floating
in colors of mauve-topaz
troupe-mahogany cadmium-jade
azure-maize teal-russet

mutating to colors of frost and sunburst
and blood-moon and glaciers and lava seething
and tide-deep fathoms and novas pulsing

the arch of incandescence hovers above
moving with the discoverers
shifting its colors
transmuting in mists of mutating hues
tinges yet unnamed
in shades outside known wavelengths

the explorers transfiguring
perpetually becoming and extending

up to the surface
up to the mountains
out to the planets
out to the stars
out to all that is
and that we can become

beyond the visible spectrum

•

The Calling

By the time of my birth, my parents had migrated from the farmlands of North Carolina and Missouri to Chicago and into a church whose members were fierce in their insistence that this was the one right way, the infallible way. On their sabbath, I attended Sunday school, church service, youth meetings, and evening service.

A copy of a painting representing Jesus hung on my bedroom wall. After we had studied the Biblical story of Samuel in Sunday school, I felt that I, too, had been called in some way into spiritual service.

Our youth group undertook outreach activities to the inner city, to skid row, where people came forward as we circled and prayed. At the county hospital, we went from room to room, seeing many who had no other visitors. Journeying to and from such activities, the youth argued about whether it was sinful to go to school and seminary to study. Did matriculation show a lack of faith in God's inspiration?

I read the Bible daily, going from cover to cover. From a small New Testament volume, I repeatedly reviewed the Sermon on the Mount.

•

Our minister sought to plunge the youth into the baptismal. He had a special Sunday aimed at *the young people*, where he reminded us that if we were not baptized that day and walked out of church

STORIES FROM A SPIRITUAL QUEST

and were hit by a car and died, we would spend eternity in hell. Our sobbing parents nor even Jesus could prevent our damnation if we did not *come forward*, he thundered, using phrases I would later encounter in reading the sermons of Jonathan Edwards.

•

One summer, at a relative's home in North Carolina, amid the old books on the shelves of the house built a century ago, I found a dusty volume about a man who decided to make his decisions by first asking himself what Jesus would do.

I began to speculate, would Jesus chew gum? Would he sleep eight hours a night? Would he eat the pigs' feet and cabbage swimming in grease in my aunt's proper kitchen? Would he tell jokes? Read comic books? Play secular songs on the piano? Have a job? Go to school? Have hobbies? Wear—what? Every action.

•

The day came when I presented the youth sermon to the whole congregation. I stood at the podium and delivered the message, that they said was just the beginning of the promise of what would come. But an event changed that onward course.

One Sunday, my adult mentors had strange looks on their faces. Hate. They breathed heavily and appeared dangerously angry. A man had come to church, and they turned him away at the door. They muttered that if he returned, they would see to it he never tried anything like this again. The gentleman with the rounded shoulders, walking slowly alone back to the street, had African ancestors. For the first time, I learned that everyone could not come into the church.

The elders insisted that the mark of Cain, who murdered brother Abel, was to be turned dark of skin by God, so that none of light skin might ever associate with his accursed descendants again. Double curse: the mark that God left on the descendants of Noah's son Ham, who laughed at his father's drunken nakedness, was also dark skin, to separate his descendants from those of light skin forever. They said we would be cast into hell eternally if we associated with those whom God has cursed, that we have no choice and could not question the will of God.

Red and yellow, black and white, all are precious in His sight, Jesus loves the little children of the world. Dissonance. How could we sing the one and be told the other?

I read my ever-present Testament, the much worn Sermon on the Mount pages. The words of Jesus pounded in my mind, that whatsoever you do to the least of these my brethren, you do also unto me. The dawning realization: they did it to Jesus. They had turned Christ away from the church.

At home, trying to piece together this discrepancy. The minister. I must talk to him. My guide. The guardian of our spiritual life. Onto my bicycle. The mile to the church. Peddling furiously. He was in the church office. I breathed heavily, awaiting his guidance, wanting him to speak for Jesus, for God, to help me understand. He looked at me. Flickered a smile. And out came the words, "Sometimes we must compromise." They blowtorched onto my brain. There were other words, saying similar things. Just don't think about it. Pray. Read the Bible. Don't take things so seriously. And compromise when necessary.

•

The following Sunday, I told my parents, dressed for church, that I could not go. I never attended there again.

Unable to get me back into church, unable to make sense of my Cain, Ham, least-of-these-brethren, what-would-Jesus-do mishmash, my parents also urged me not to take things so seriously. But I did not know how the phrase applied. If heaven, hell, eternity, right and wrong, salvation, and God were not to be taken seriously, what was? What alternatives was I supposed to see? Had I not been taught there was one right way?

•

On the heels of this, I encountered my first science class. The church had insisted that evolution was wrong, explaining that if man had descended from monkeys, then when a monkey lived long enough, it would turn into a man.

The church had also taught that because God created Eve from Adam's rib, all males to this day still had one less rib than women. They scoffed at those who ignored these obvious proofs.

In science class. With a skeleton displayed in the corner of the room. Do men have one less rib? Then came the revelation: males and females have the same number. And Darwin didn't say aging monkeys turn into humans.

If my former mentors were wrong about this and wrong about who could come into the church, what else were they wrong about? Which parts of my whole life structure were accurate and which not? And how was I to know? If parts of the standards I had been taught were faulty, by what other standards could I screen them? And what or who was wrong—the Bible? ministers? elders? parents? me? Where along the chain of information had a break occurred? Or maybe they just compromised. Maybe they just did not take it seriously. I stared at the picture on the bedroom wall. Did you compromise? Did you take things too seriously?

For the gaining of a rib and a refused admittance to church, chunks of absolute belief were falling from my Sunday school room ceiling, my church roof, the sky, as the vault of heaven came raining down in pieces. If Jesus could not attend the church I grew up in, then where did he dwell?

•

Somewhere, out there, at the same time, a man named Joseph Campbell, of whom I would learn later, was writing *The Hero With A Thousand Faces*. As I was being sundered in some strange way from the perspectives of my family and church, he was describing global cultural myths of humans severed from the familiar, cast into the wilderness, trying to find the way to the mystic union. Life shattered that it could be reborn.

It was no hero, but a solitary youth who set out to find the epiphany. At twelve, I determined to explore for myself all religions, denominations, sects, cults, and philosophies of the world possible. In a muddled way, with no plan of action, I ventured forth to attempt somehow to investigate every religious perspecive on earth.

Not another person in the world did I know with whom to speak of the quest. Was I taking all this far too seriously, not knowing how to compromise? The universe I had known changed forever.

•

That intention intertwined with a previous school episode. In the early grades, one of our class and his family had come from Germany. During the Second World War, several parents talked about them as *the enemy*. Some of the class, his friends until then, caught him after everyone else had left late one afternoon and tied him to a schoolyard tree, stoned him, urinated on him, leaving him bound, hysterical, and brutalized. He and his family disappeared into the night. The horror crept into my life that anyone's peers could label and attack them. With whom could any of us ultimately be safe, awaiting a label of some kind and an attack. Where on earth could I find the path to inner spiritual development to so influence behavior that it would prevent people from doing this?

•

I did not want to be a part of an ethnicity, a race, a category set against other categories, a tribe opposing other tribes, an in-group opposing the out-groups. I wanted to become human.

The Bus

While in grade school, I wrote a column of book reviews for our suburban paper. In our high school's publication, I also reviewed books in a weekly column, *Just Browsing*. Books provided available resources for delving into religions. While I valued the written accounts, on my quest I wanted to hear the stories of individuals' worldviews in their own voices, to somehow find a way to talk with people across the country, most of which, for me, remained *terra incognita*.

•

As a freshman at Denison University, my courses included a class in Children's Theater. We rehearsed plays and then took them by bus, with props and costumes, to school auditoriums for their assemblies. On the way, I saw the hills and roads and small towns, a fragment of my *terra incognita*.

From the theater bus experiences, a plan materialized. I had no money to own a car or for plane fare, but bus travel was cheap. I could go to another state or two over Christmas vacation, spring recess, and part of the summer. Then I could see for myself the rural and urban centers and meet people and hear their stories.

I purchased round trip tickets; packed a minimalist bag, including packages of peanuts and jerky. Assured of returning and having survival nourishment, I slept overnight on the coach and in stations. Tickets permitted layovers at any stop, to continue on a later bus.

•

People. Now the stories started. Bus conversations, late into
the night, with other solitary travelers, seated together by
chance. The voices in twangs, accents, and dialects telling their
tales of marriages, divorces, funerals, lost jobs, illnesses—the rut
of life happening.

Moods radiated from every tree outline, every grain field, every
farmhouse with its shutters and shingles telling of those who built
it, and from cramped alleys of cities where the buses stabled, amid
the smell of sewers and blowing refuse. I watched the huts along
corn rows, seeming to see the boundaries of visions of people
sitting on porches, or children playing in ditches, or tired field
workers. I saw my own boundaries in them, the borders of our
thinking, and wanted to stretch those barriers, erase them, letting
us all migrate toward the unknown together.

•

Books also were my fellow travelers. My eyes would survey the
level flats of Oklahoma, the trees all leaning away from the ever-
present wind, and then shift down to the page where Ahab
clomped the decks and peered amid the waves to see the albino
symbol of his destiny. Authors of the centuries became my
companions through the switchback turns in the Rockies, and
across the velvet rank of the Dismal Swamp. The biographies and
autobiographies such as those of Albert Schweitzer, Mahatma
Gandhi, Saint Teresa, and George Washington Carver came
forth between Boise and Cheyenne. Reference works on
philosophies, religions, denominations, sects, and cults joined me
through Maine and Rhode Island.

•

The information from books and people blended. I read of the
religion of Zoroaster and mused through the hills of South
Dakota about the descriptions of the eternal flame kept burning
in the temples. Chancing upon a visiting Zoroastrian, I asked

about the symbol of the flame. He laughed, saying he had no idea, that any meaning was probably lost in antiquity, but if I found out, to let him know.

•

Under the tutelage of an astute oral interpretation professor at the University of Arizona, to which I had transferred, she affirmed that the spoken text marked the epitome of cultural experience, as we explored the roots of humanity and performed the refined distillations. We sought to bring alive, in voice, the poetry of the ages, essays, short stories, and cuttings of entire novels and plays. "To California," she told me one day. "You are ready. I have entered you into the regional communication competitions. Prepare to leave for Los Angeles." A destination. A journey between holidays. So a mutation in the bus traveling pattern emerged, with more soon to come.

•

The same professor, calling me again into her office, explained that she could not attend a club meeting where she was to present an evening of readings and was sending me in her stead. Thus my classroom and contest readings became programs.

Other classes: the history of rhetoric. Who outside academia would care about the sequence of theorists? Other groups did, I found, as the faculty recommended me to those who requested presentations. Topics also came from chance encounters, remarks about the Sufis or Mithraism or the Druids. So emerged themes related to worldviews and communication. These topics joined my repertoire.

People at the local meetings, visiting from another city, extended an invitation to travel to their location to make presentations, followed by other invitations within the state and then outside the state, on weekends and holidays, in a network of people who knew people, and organizations who wanted speakers.

The organizations volunteered overnight hospitality. My *terra incognita* increasingly had homes and people. I was suffused in a variety of economic, educational, professional, regional, family, and religious perspectives. I was hearing their stories. This odyssey had an energy of its own.

•

A host family living in a sumptuous gated community drove me to their virtual palace. When they took me inside for the night, I expected lavish furnishings, but found only fruit crates and throw pillows. They built houses they could not afford, selling each in turn, moving from one to the next, with improvised furniture and improvised lives.

•

In Washington state, my host took me to the shores of the Pacific where a tribal chief, a lifetime fisherman, spoke of the dolphins galloping along the waves like herds of horses. He made descriptive motions with his hands that spoke a graceful language of their own. I stood with totem pole makers who, with their tools and explanations, extracted the stories embedded in the wood.

•

In Michigan, a visitor from Canada drew me aside after a presentation and invited me to talk to a group in his town during the summer. I accepted. Someone in a neighboring town asked for presentations there. The Canadian travel eventually reached from the Atlantic to the Pacific, three thousand miles across the continent, in homes with people with stories.

•

Individuals kindly referred me to friends to stay with as I traveled, including New York City. The friend answered the door. I stood there with my bag, after fifteen hundred miles by bus. "I'm on my way to work," he said offhandedly. "Here's the key. Use whatever's in the refrigerator. See you whenever."

I explored from this basepoint during the day. He led me through the back streets after work, one night, coming up from the subway, emerging into an eerie nether world of darkness, a blackout.

•

In the western uplands, I stopped at the family farm of another student I knew at the university. "Thee are welcome to be here. We will show thee the farm." And the Quakers shared their life experiences.

•

In an Indian village atop a mesa, I sat in a kiva and listened to the chief review tribal prophecies, as a desert storm thundered outside. The chief pointed at what he said were old blood stains on the kiva walls. "The missionaries of Jesus came into this holy place and beat our people, spattering blood on the walls, and threatened them with death if they did not convert to the way of Christ. We have never washed away the bloodstains so the children will not forget. We had no curse words in our language until then. Now we do." He repeated the names of the missionaries' denominations.

Afterward, we watched children playing basketball without keeping score, explaining they all played on the same team, and everyone always won.

•

There were bus alternatives. In graduate school as part of my fellowship, I served as a debate coach, rehearsed the teams, and led excursions to tournaments in Illinois and Indiana and Pennsylvania. Our transportation was an outdated black hearse with oval windows. The space where caskets had once rested became leg room for students sitting on the benches built on either side, facing each other.

The undergraduates perfected hearse-mirth in several scenarios. In their favorite, the students leaned away from the oval windows, while one of them, lying on the bench below, would raise a hand, all that could be seen through the glass, and scratch zombie-like down the pane, leaving the outside watchers wide-eyed.

•

Headed toward the bus station for one of the invited-to-speak weekends, I met another student who said he did not need his car for a couple of days and urged me to use it. The miles rolled by, as the gas gauge circled to "E." At the service station, I realized how well disguised some gas tank openings can be, not finding it in any of the usual places. It finally appeared under a lifted section of taillight. Cruising on down the highway, I met the barrier of circling blue lights. The station owner had notified the police of a driver who could not find the gas tank of what must be a stolen car.

•

Another long bus ride in the darkness. An anonymous seat companion in the night told of soap-opera-like happenings in his life. Suddenly he shifted in the shadows and said, "Hey, where you from? Your voice don't have no accent. Don't sound like you from nowhere."

•

After I had spoken, my host, a St. Louis woman, ushered me into her large home. She and her three children were fountains of articulate interchange. She said, "It's a pity you won't meet my husband, though I told him of you. He doesn't talk to people anymore. A mid-life crisis. He's troubled, searching for a new identity." She poured coffee. "We're ancestrally Jewish, but nothing he knows satisfies him now or answers his questions." She pointed up the carpeted curving staircase. "Stays up there in his room. We take him up his food. He owns the business and lets other people run it." She shrugged. "He'll work it out in time."

As I turned back toward the table, the eyes of the children looked past me, toward the stairs. A foot appeared from the second story landing, finding its position on the top step. Slowly there came into view the legs, robe-wrapped torso, shoulders, and head of the recluse. "Oh," whispered the woman. "He's coming down! He hasn't been down for ever so long. He wants to meet you! You should be so honored! He's brilliant." His descent looked like a scene from Sunset Boulevard as he walked toward me with an expressionless face.

"I am but a poor and ignorant man, seeking to understand," he said. "Please, let me ask you questions so you can elucidate for me." He began with rabbinical traditions. "Could you tell me what the great teacher of the seventeenth century meant when he said…" Following it with, "Might he have meant—not that I understand, you see, I am only seeking illumination from the wise—that the tradition of which he spoke was intended…" His rapt family clung to his every word. Norma Desmond was shape-shifting into Columbo doing his feigned-ignorance interrogations.

•

The demure woman dressed in high society garb picked me up at the bus station to drive toward downtown Seattle. As she explained the itinerary leading up to my presentation at the Women's Association club room, suddenly a car pulled too abruptly in front of us. She lowered the window and bellowed out in a sandpaper voice a lexicon of profanity, accompanied with a range of Italian street gestures. She raised the window and continued, in her previously sweet voice, to recite the schedule. She added, with soft, precise articulation, "One must let out one's feelings immediately and not let them accumulate inside. Better for him to deal with them than me."

•

"I used to be a blues singer of the red hot mama variety, in bars, an alcoholic, and a lot more," said my host and driver. "I'm still a bleached blond and overweight, but sober." She drove toward an Indian reservation to meet her friends, explaining that when her life had reached its nadir, she experienced a transcendental moment, gave up her former ways, and sought to help Native Americans. She used her musicality to create songs about the history, leaders, and traditions of the tribe.

The people gathered around her like a folk hero in a home we visited. A piano beckoned her. Her girth bounced and her hands danced on the keys, as her raspy voice ground out her original songs about chieftains' visions to a rhythm and blues beat.

•

My host couple made pottery and lived in a desert adobe home. Tables stood laden with their handiwork in various stages of shaping, drying, baking, and glazing as their child played on a throw rug. Something moved across the bare wooden floor. A clump of hairy legs and body. A large tarantula.

"Oh, there he is," the mother said, picking it up and letting it walk up her arm. "He's part of the family. Keeps the pests down." She stroked its back. "The stories about their venom are exaggerated." And she set it down gently to continue on its way across the room. "We have to be careful not to drop them. Their legs pop off easily. We must live in harmony with nature."

•

A couple, who defined themselves as evangelical atheists, held regular meetings, actively proselytizing, to convert people to their religion, explaining that they wanted to save them from wasting their lives on old legends and get on with the true religion of helping others.

•

In Florida in a host home, I met an accountant by day, who had created a strange room at home, boarding up the windows, installing fully mirrored walls, and in this dark space, hung strings of tiny, barely visible lights from floor to ceiling, reflecting in all directions to infinity. He sat cross legged on a cushion in the middle in the near darkness. We talked into the night about his life's search in his room full of stars.

•

The Detroit priest hosted me in his over-the-store rooms in a decaying section of town. A mirror-ebony-surfaced grand piano stood like a museum display in the middle of the room. He performed with the touch of a professional. "Religions? You want to know about religions? Let me tell you." And he poured out experiences of what really happened in the lives of the clerics, beyond the pulpit, behind the scenes. He saw celibacy as a two thousand year old public relations ploy, advertising without substance. For several hundred years in the early church, all priests and bishops married, leaving their land to their children. The church wanted them to leave it to the institution. So they ordained celibacy and inherited vast land holdings. Jesus probably married. The gospels that said so were suppressed. His hands flurried across the keys in a Chopin prelude.

•

The Dean of a Baptist Seminary invited me to come into the walls of their learning, and to tell them something of my search so far. The bus carried me across three states to get there. "Tell us of your findings," he said. I looked at the faces of the seminarians. Here I could have been sitting, studying, a novitiate myself. I thought of my calling that might have brought me to a place like this. Instead, I had become a story listener, a crumpled mass of wrinkled clothing huddled on midnight buses peering out at the lights of farm windows and sleeping towns. Now the seminarians addressed me as a story teller, a wanderer who had seen sights and heard sounds, brought into the cloistered walls to speak of the search.

•

Somehow, in the cracks of time between the life of university classes, I had traveled the landscape, ocean to ocean, from the Gulf of Mexico through Canada, to every continental state but one and every province but one. I harbored feelings accumulated from viewing sharecroppers huts and metropolitan monoliths, and listened to ideas mixed from a patchwork of conversations, a marathon of perspectives, and sipped from attar of solitude and nectar of dialogue. I was being baptized in stories, on my quest.

Humanity

The impact of the childhood events of the man turned away from the church and the grade school student attacked by his peers was repeated as other experiences revealed people responding to their fellow humans as categories instead of individuals. As a high school student, studying at home, I placed traded pictures of other students on my desk. My father came up behind me, reached over and removed one, saying it would not be appropriate for anyone to see a photo in our home of someone of another race.

Experiences blended into a realization. If the man denied admittance to the church was Jesus excluded from the church, then we had all been excluded. If my grade school student had been tied to a tree, so had we all. If my father removed my friend's picture, he removed all of us. There palpitated within me the awareness that we are of one blood, thee and I, and what is done to one is done to me, to us all. I hoped to express my spiritual search through efforts for human and civil rights for everyone.

•

As I approached the completion of my Ph.D. degree at Ohio University, I wanted to find a teaching position in the South, at the start of the Sixties. Demonstrations for equal rights grew. I wished to be in the middle of whatever was happening. With my training in communication, I hoped to use the background to help bring people together to talk, instead of the violent alternatives that filled newspapers headlines.

My job application forms all had a blank for race on them. I put H for Human. Making me immediately suspect.

The dean of an African-American state school to which I had applied in a segregated Southern region wrote of my acceptance for the position and asked for a photo, a state requirement. After receiving it, he replied that he was sorry we live in a world where he must tell me, having received my picture, that I could not work there. The legislature would immediately cut their funding and close the school if they hired me. Perhaps, he wrote, in some brighter time in the future, people such as you and me will be able to meet or even work together.

Acquaintances, knowing my intentions, made contact with some non-public institutions they knew of, and I received and accepted a job offer for which I had not applied, at a private African-American college.

My African-American friends at Ohio University all came from northern states and had said repeatedly that they would never go to the South. They congratulated me on the job choice and held a gathering of farewell. One lingered after the others left. He reaffirmed that he would never venture below the Mason-Dixon line. He tried to formulate something he wanted to say, prefacing it with the statement that he would never see me again so long as I lived down there, and then added, "Take care of my people."

Last item before leaving Ohio, Ph.D. granting. My parents came for the graduation ceremony. When they realized the nature of the school at which I would work, they said it would probably have been better if I had never been born.

An Ohio faculty advisor, one I considered an understanding friend, called me to his office. He told me I was throwing away my degree taking the job I had accepted, and that his institution's resources had been wasted on me.

•

In my new position in Tennessee, along with working on campus, I lived there as well, in the African-American community. Bus boycotts, sit-ins, demonstrations, marches, selective buying. The students were in the middle of it. On some days, in a class of thirty, only a few were there, the rest having been jailed for requesting service at a lunch counter.

My days were spent in classes, office hours, and grading papers. But the nights and weekends were crowded with planning meetings for the next activities, the next strategy to counter the responses of the hate groups. Students voluntarily took turns keeping watch at night by the civil rights leader's home, to sound an alert in case of attempted shootings or bombings.

•

I went to buy some furniture at a downtown store. They cordially accommodated me and worked out my short term payments and arranged a delivery time. Instead of delivery, that afternoon I received a curt phone call from the store telling me that when they realized where I worked and lived, they had permanently cancelled any possibility of credit purchases for me.

•

There had been no breakthroughs yet to discussions, until the wives of faculty at a neighboring denominational school, all Euro-American, quietly contacted the civil rights leaders to ask to talk. Two of my African-American colleagues were going and invited me to go with them to the home of one of the wives.

Her shades were drawn. Our arrival was quick, as we were hurried in, the door hastily closed after looks up and down the street. They asked if we were followed.

Inside, only women awaited us. They explained that the males could not participate or their jobs could be at risk at their denominational school. So they were establishing alibis elsewhere. If need be, they could claim not knowing what their wives were doing.

The women were tense, searching for words to say. The hostess served tea. The cups and saucers rattled in trembling hands like an orchestra of dishes. The first questions: Why are you people doing this? Why are you disrupting our town? What do you people want? The answers, equality of opportunity, the same treatment. An undercurrent of dissonance, and then the phone rang. A wife had a call from a baby-sitter. Sick child. For a magic moment, the confronting races become parents and talk slipped easily to children, their sicknesses, family matters. A shock of similarities. A first step toward reality.

From these timorous efforts, we slowly created multiple groups meeting around the city, interracially, discussing what everyone called *the problem*. The opportunity came to use my communication training, to encourage the dialogue of what it means to be human.

•

On weekends, I drove with African-American colleagues on all night journeys to New Orleans, Jackson, Birmingham, cities across the South, to meet with gatherings of civil rights workers there, offering mutual help. No motel stops along the way. None were integrated. No restaurants. Few rest rooms.

A water fountain in the town square, formerly marked *white only*, had the sign removed. My students assisted an aged lady to walk up to the fountain, to drink from it for the first time.

Medgar Evers came from Mississippi to speak. I sat on the platform with him and stayed up late afterwards as he spoke of what had to be done despite the dangers. Before the year was out, he was murdered in his driveway.

•

The civil rights leaders explained that they needed me to go into the segregated restaurant as a spotter to witness events during a sit-in, in case testimony was needed later for court appeals. I sat in the cafe and sipped tea awaiting the arrival of my students, but I was to show no signs of recognition nor intervene, only observe and become a potential witness.

The students arrived peacefully, simply to order a meal. The owner grabbed a cattle prod. My students, who earlier in the day were discussing world literature in our class, were thrown to the floor and beaten and stung with electric shocks and lay writhing in pain. The police arrived and arrested the youths for disturbing the peace.

As times changed, police response became less predictable. In Atlanta, in an apartment at an interracial gathering, a mob formed outside, pelting the walls with stones. The mob called the police to get us. The police came, but unexpectedly held the mob back briefly, shouting to us to try to escape since there was nothing else they could do to help us. Some of our group ran toward the darkness at the other end of the alley. The predatory mob broke through the police lines.

•

The African-American civil rights leaders readied to leave for a meeting called by city officials and other members of the Euro-American community to be held for the first time in a Euro-American church building. However, the white organizers had stipulated that I was not welcome in any white church and could not attend. I felt kinship to the man turned away from my childhood church.

•

We talked with occupants of tent city. When African-American sharecroppers had tried to exercise the right to vote, land owners had evicted them, people stranded between the past and the future. They stayed in tents in fields, as cars drove by at night, shooting into the canvas coverings, with men, women, and children inside.

•

After a full work day on campus, a car load of us drove miles on the country roads to backwoods farms. We were assisting with the Martin Luther King literacy project. They dropped me off at a farm home, and the car drove on to take others to other rural houses. A seventy-five year old came home from the field. I worked with him to help him learn to read. He and I slowly deciphered newspaper headlines. A word here. Another there. A smile like a sunburst. I was the only non-African-American working with the project in that area. He told me I was the first person of my background ever to be in his home, with whom he had ever had a conversation. The car returned, we made the rounds of dirt roads, picking up the others as midnight neared. A sheriff's car began to follow us.

•

Two of us, an interracial pair, on a deserted Georgia road, drove from yet another weekend meeting late at night. A single vehicle came speeding up behind us, bright lights on, and saw who we were. A jarring impact. Another one. They rammed us, pushing the car forward, bumper to bumper, trying to force us off the road. With a roar and a thud, our car reeled. In a rush of tires and clouds of dust, their car veered off onto a dirt side road and screamed into the darkness.

•

A saintly man, this minister of Euro-American background, with a shock of white hair. I saw wisdom in his eyes. He had come from the North to live as he thought Jesus wanted him to, in a rural African-American community in the South, to help with voter registration, to try to bridge the gaps, to reach out to all the children of God.

After his African-American parishioners left one Sunday morning following the service, he lingered to close up. Those who also called themselves Christians and in the name of Jesus supported segregation, came when he was alone. They left him for dead, a bloody heap on the dust outside his church door.

•

I was requested to dine, my inviter said, in a *white home*. Be grateful, came the unsmiling admonition, that they risk their reputation to even have you there.

•

In the midst of what felt often like a battlefield of civil rights activities, I received a letter from an African-American friend with whom I had been in school in Ohio, who had refused to ever come South. He had gone more northerly instead and had become a minister. He went to what he described as a combat zone of inner city Chicago to begin his ministry. He wanted me to come during my school's spring break to *walk with him*. "They haven't seen one of you here in the parish where I work," he said. "Come and walk with me."

I went. He looked fight-fatigued himself, thinner, wearing his black garb and cleric collar, too wide now that he had lost weight. He walked me through the rooms of housing projects, pointed out the drug dealers lounging in the debris-strewn hallways, stepped over naked babies crying in their own filth on the concrete walks, knocked on doors with multiple locks and chains.

"Stay by me," he said, "and you should be safe." This from the person who had a local radio program emphasizing racial harmony, for which, he told me, some of his *brothers* had seen fit to threaten his life. And twice already he described being robbed, beaten, and rolled in the gutter on these rounds.

He comforted the sick who had no family nor health care. Stood with a pregnant thirteen-year-old staring comatose out the window. Spoke with the woman with no more tears left after her third son had died, this one shot down at her front door lying in a pool of his own blood. My friend's rounds, his ministry.

He stayed in the remnants of the old parsonage connected

to the church. Bars tried to protect the windows and doors that had not already been broken in and boarded over. The smell of decay and waste pervaded everything. He had no staff. The remaining parishioners, the aged, the unemployed, the homeless, the surviving youth, had little income for donations. Denominational headquarters had planned to close the church to cut their loses, when he had implored them to let him try. They told him it was hopeless, that the church was dead and the ghetto was rotting. The idealist had replied that the souls were alive and needed help. They gave him a little while longer to try.

After I had spoken to his congregation earlier in the evening, the two of us sat at midnight in the decaying parsonage with sirens wailing somewhere in the distance, He said, "I want to introduce the arts—music, painting, literature, drama. To feed our spirits. All I need are funds, space, support, and time." He smiled at the irony, through his chronic exhaustion.

He, in his war zone of the inner city; I, from the front lines of the South. We talked into the night like battle-fatigued veterans looking back on a career of combat. We were in our twenties and wanted to change the world.

•

I boarded a bus after a civil rights conference in another state to ride overnight back to my campus, where I had an early class to teach the next morning. Weary in the late night, all I wanted was to find a seat and sleep. But the bus was electric with strangeness. People were standing in the dark aisle, although I could see a vacant seat in the middle.

While buses had recently integrated, in theory, changing the back and front dichotomy, individual attitudes varied. There was only one African-American on board, sitting where for so long the law had not permitted. Beside him, the empty seat. Around him, murmuring, looks of anger. I sat in the empty seat, pushed off sleep, to talk. To do a normal thing. To converse with another human being. For all the activities, all the demonstrations and negotiations were for this, for two humans to communicate. He looked startled. Replied cautiously. People leaned into the aisles trying to catch our words.

We talked through the night. Once he found out where I worked, he asked incessant questions about what I was doing, about civil rights involvement. A strange intensity shaded his words. Sleepless, I departed the bus at dawn as he continued on.

Weeks passed. One morning, as I walked down the college corridor toward my classroom, I saw a familiar face, the rider on the bus. "Thought you'd stand out, and I wouldn't have any trouble finding you," he smiled.

He told me in short neutral phrases that he had worked in civil rights activities too, supporting King's non-violence. But acquaintances had gotten to him, reached his emotions, saying those methods would never work. They taunted him, asking if he had personally ever met one white man who was *all right*. He admitted no. And he left the projects he was working on and took a bus to join with a militant group advocating violence and separation. That had been the night of our journey together. He said that the next day he had returned to work with King's group.

•

Movie theaters were segregated. Since I went to no theaters, restaurants, or other public places if they were unavailable to everyone, I saw virtually no films for years. Until, after demonstrations and negotiations, the first theater in the region opened to integrated seating in a city an hour's drive away, keeping the process as quiet as possible. Four of us drove over. Owners and ushers had practiced the drill of trying to look natural while rushing our little integrated group in and seating us quickly. With eye-darting alertness, they anticipated problems. We watched *Lawrence of Arabia*. Every sound from the auditorium caused glances away from the camels galloping out of desert mirages on the screen.

•

From the northern states and Canada I received invitations to talk about what they referred to as firsthand experiences in the civil rights activities.

In Halifax, Nova Scotia, I addressed a meeting where a Euro-Canadian said to that no such problems existed in Canada, that everything was totally equal for all. An Afro-Canadian in the audience caught my eye, flickering a knowing smile to see her afterward. She took me to her home and called in family and friends. "Now," she said, "we're going to tell it like it really is here."

After I had returned to the campus from speaking in several cities, the college president called me into his office. He cleared his throat and began, "As a black man, it is difficult for me to tell you what I am now forced to." My efforts were commendable, he said, from his personal perspective. But as head of the institution, he had to be sensitive to public opinion. "I have received calls from white people who have heard from acquaintances as far away as Canada that you had spoken favorably there about integration." They had insisted that he warn me, and if necessary, terminate my position.

•

There were moments of mirth. Segregationists said that racial mixing would lead to mongrelization. One night, riding in the back seat of a car with an African-American lady, I chanced to be holding, wrapped in a blanket, a sleeping little puppy that one of the front-seat passengers had newly acquired and was taking home. We stopped for gas at one of those dark small town pumps with three rest rooms, marked *men*, *women*, and *colored*. The attendant was obviously upset by the apparent interracial couple in back and kept trying to see the child in the blanket. After we had filled and paid, I lifted the flap covering the dog's face. The attendant stood aghast, his worst fears realized, a mongrel! As we sped off.

•

I received a phone call from the president of another African-American college, in Little Rock, inviting me to take a job as academic dean in the late 1960s. In my new position in Arkansas, I attended meetings of academic administrators from other colleges, where my institution was just beginning to be included. In our rounds of initial introductions, there was often a silence after mine. I served on an accreditation team where the chairperson, representing a major state university, refused to speak to me during eight hours of activities.

•

A phone call came from a person who identified himself as being from the white section of Little Rock, who was an educated and socially liberal person that associated with others like himself. They had heard of the white administrator at the black school, and invited me to meet with them. When I did, they asked questions about what black people thought and how black people felt and what black attitudes were on a multitude of issues. I questioned why they asked me. But we don't know any of them, they said.

•

The Great Society programs gushed money for consortia between traditionally African-American and traditionally Euro-American schools. Usually the former applicants were in Southern states, and the latter, Northern. The president of my college and the head of a northern school gingerly approached the possibility of such a mutual grant proposal by phone. They agreed to head a delegation from each school to meet at a neutral city conference center midway between their cities to explore the issues involved and work out a detailed proposal.

My college president was apprehensive. He desperately wanted this to work out. But he expressed serious concern with going himself or sending anyone else of his race, afraid they would somehow say the wrong thing and jinx the effort. "You know how your people think and how to talk to them," he told me, "so I'm sending you by yourself." He flew me off alone to the half-way city where the meeting was to take place, leaving me to explain my solo appearance.

I registered at the hotel, cleaned up, put on my business suit, and walked toward the conference room that has been reserved. I entered first and waited in the empty chamber. A few minutes later, the door hesitantly opened. In came, not the expected delegation, but a solitary person, an African-American. We looked at each other, and, as it to dawned on us what had happened, we began to laugh.

His school had hired him as their first minority administrator. His president desperately wanted this affiliation, but was fearful that some of them would say the wrong thing and botch the efforts. You know how to talk to your people, had been the words sending this other single negotiator on his way.

We said almost simultaneously, "Let's do it all." "Yes." "Everything possible under the grant." So it was settled instantly, and we two delegations went chuckling away from the sterile board chamber, to a restaurant, to share our experiences.

•

I was mowing the lawn in the African-American neighborhood in Little Rock where I lived. A woman not of the neighborhood drove around the block several times, more slowly each time and looking increasingly angry, finally stopping her car. She said emotionally that I was risking the eternal damnation of my soul by going against the teachings of Jesus Christ by living with those people, when God, in the Bible, specifically ordered separation.

•

I received a call in my office from a local alumnus of Ohio University who had seen my name in the alumni directory and wanted to take me out for lunch to meet his friends. He came to the work address, only then realizing it was an African-American school. He said, "I had no idea who you were when I called. Under the circumstances, we cannot have lunch together. I can't afford to be seen with you in public." As he exited, he added, "You know, you could almost pass for white."

•

My quest for exploring spiritual perspectives had become inseparably combined with behavior toward other people. The two could not be divided. Not by veering off to speculative theology, administrative infallibility, scriptural canonizing, ritual, creation stories, after-life speculations, or any of the other subsets, could this measure of religion be minimized or margin-noted. What did all the other aspects connected with religion ultimately produced in the behavior of one human being toward another? Perhaps someday we can all pass—as human.

Religion Querist

Gleanings from the religious readings that had become part of my exploration since high school: Pope Hormisdas' son, Silverius, succeeded his father as Pope. Pope Paul IV developed the Index of Forbidden Books. Pope Clement XII failed as a Pope, according to some, but received commendation building the Trevi Fountain in Rome.

If the word Catholic meant Universal, why call it the *Roman* Catholic church? To differentiate it from the American Catholic Church, Christ Catholic Church, Christ Catholic Exarchate of Americas and Europe, and the North American Old Roman Catholic Church.

And the Baptists—German Baptists, Norwegian Baptists, Italian Baptists, Swedish Baptists, and Korean Baptists. In 1814, the Triennial Baptist had formed, including most U.S. congregations. But in 1845, because of differences over whether God permitted slavery or not, the southern brethren separated and formed the Southern Baptists. By 1907, the others called themselves the Northern Baptist Convention, but changed that in 1950 to the American Baptists. And the Christian Unity Baptist Association, the Duck River and Kindred Association of Baptists, the…

•

As a student in Arizona, I surveyed the organizational list on campus. The Amerind Club. American Indians and friends.

Joining in, I met students of many tribal designations. And with each, religious backgrounds. A Hopi friend assured me with calm simplicity that Hopi meant peaceful, and if the world would follow that way of life, it would be at peace.

On campus resided a wealth of international students. I sought out those of Islamic background and individually asked questions of people from Egypt, Syria, Saudi Arabia, Turkey, Iraq, Iran, the Emirates, Jordan, and more. Their lengthy responses included concern about the variety of ways their religion was practiced in other countries. Several urged differentiating between the religion and the cultural practices of Muslim countries, emphasizing the two were often confused.

•

"Who cares?" another student said to me, swigging his tequila. "Why do you waste your time? Angels, devils, gods, clergy, belief in this, belief in that. Why do you bother?" I looked around his room at the piles of blueprints, diagrams, and drawings, spread on every available table and pinned to the walls. His engineering thesis involved the design of an entire ramp system for a planned highway interchange. He worked around the clock, napping at intervals, rushing out at any time of day or night to pace and measure some needed distance at the site. Stacks of reference books and pages of notes rose from the floor. "Why do you do this?" I asked. "Because I have to!" he said. "So do I," I answered.

•

Huppah: the canopy beneath which a wedding ceremony in Judaism takes place.

Marcion: the theologian aesthetic who expounded on the Gnostic perspective in Rome and Asia Minor about 150 C.E.

Shaivism: religious practices and institutions related to the Hindu deity Shiva.

Chang Tao Ling in the second century C.E. , the first Heavenly Master of the Heavenly Master group of religious Taoism. In visions he said he met Lao Tzu who had lived seven hundred years before. Developing means of prolonging life, he used his long span to create what was called The Great Peace on earth.

•

Pope John Paul I was the first Pope in a thousand years to refuse the crown of the triple tiara, and held office for only 33 days, the shortest pontificate.

Pope Pius IX served the longest, more than thirty-one years. He called the first Vatican Council, that voted, after prolonged argument, on Papal infallibility. A newspaper reported that a group of old men in a hot room in summer Rome, after most of the opposition had walked out, voted one of their number to be without error.

•

A century-old religious group held a meeting in Los Angeles, to attract newcomers to the dawn of the new age, the coming of the new messiah. I sat in the loft room to hear this proclamation and then to see the speaker pantomime the riding of a stick horse and perform a falsetto soliloquy in the character of Witch Hazel, dedicated to the glory of God and his kingdom on earth.

•

"What are your teachings on transformation?" I asked the groups I visited. For this was the passion for me beyond their meetings to convert, beyond the ritual music and chants, beyond the collections and testimonials.

As the number of worldviews I studied continued growing, these discoveries came into conversations with another student preparing to go into professional church work. She tensely told me she was taking me somewhere as a surprise. At her destination, a sign on the building identified it as the national headquarters of her religious organization. We were ushered into the board room.

Waiting were a group of conservatively dressed, suave-voiced men with intonations of the pulpit coloring their phrases. They began an interrogation about my private journey, pointing out that when you have encountered truth already, you show lack of faith by continuing to search. There was, they emphasized, only one right way.

•

The Greek Orthodox priest patted me paternalistically on the arm. "My son," he said, "I must give you advice." He, in his robes, found the right place in his bifocals to look at me in this close position, his chin thrust up into the air. He had asked about my church home. I had indicated that in the past year I had visited many groups, and he asked me to list them. His brow furrowed. He leaned closer, bifocaling me, chin way up now, and repeated the name of one of the groups. "You must not consider them. They have no theology. No THEO-logy. You must not go there."

•

I talked with practitioners about their fasting, prayer vigils, the discipline of yoga, the use of specialized diets. While a student, I read in the yellow-backed tome written by Gandhi, of his attempts to simplify his life. Part of his practice was to reduce his food intake to four basic items. I experimented with his menu. Finally an acquaintance, on the way to school, lunch neatly packed for later consumption, delivered to me an identical package of greasy, salty, fat-filled, condiment-topped offerings, to rescue me from Gandhi.

•

1307-1312, the Knights Templar, faithful servants of the Lord, were systematically burned at the stake and exterminated by the Christian government of France.

Mishnah concerns the oral code of law developed mainly in the two centuries before the Great Revolt, by the Pharisees, the liberals who abolished slavery ahead of their contemporary societies.

The Sabeans were a group who existed in the southwestern Arabian peninsula at least five hundred B.C.E. in the kingdom referred to in the Bible as Sheba.

Prajna, a term used by Buddhists for inner wisdom and insight in relation to enlightenment.

Rites of passage. Perhaps existing from antiquity, but only so named in 1909 by Arnold van Gennep as a category of ritual.

•

The medicine wheel, a native American explained, was round like the horizon. Marked by the four directions: the rising sun, the setting sun, the cold north, the warmer south. Each with a totem creature, each with a color. Each with a human trait. The mouse in the south, close to the ground, seeing only details, micro-managing. The eagle of the north, gliding high, seeing vastly the system of hills, valleys and streams below. Born in one spot on the wheel, the human should circle it, becoming whole, complete.

•

More churches in America: Assyrian Church of the East. Eastern Orthodox Catholic Church in America. Greek Orthodox Archdiocese of North and South America. The Holy Ukrainian Autocephalic Orthodox Church in Exile.

•

In one religious organization that sought to absorb all others, I had found a series of steps in their scriptures that promised enlightenment. To my query as to where the study groups meet that peruse, analyze, and behaviorize these guidelines, a member looked at me sadly for my lack of understanding. He explained they have no need to discuss these. These are directions for the non-members, the seekers after truth. When they join, they have found all truth and that is the culmination of illumination. Then all they have to do is obey without question the administration. Had the pathway to illumination been detoured toward obedience to bureaucrats?

•

In the northeastern United States, I heard the tale of Deganawidah. Centuries ago, he taught the process of inner peace and its expression outwardly to bring native nations together. His concepts merged together the Six Nations Iroquois Confederacy, uniting states before America was so named.

•

While my exploration continued through books and North American journeys, more lay beyond.

Beyond the Borders

In my continuing quest to talk with people of perspectives around the world, I needed to go beyond the borders of one continent, to hear the stories of people of other countries. The next phase came when I accepted a teaching position at the University of Arkansas at Little Rock. I received an invitation to speak at a conference in Austria. The border now had a portal, and I walked onto the streets of Vienna, conversing with conferees from multiple cultures.

The professional opportunities multiplied. My field of communication related to virtually everything, and studies beckoned. Projects grew themselves, with seeds of ideas dropping off of the presentation in Austria to take root the next year in Budapest, Hungary, to spring up in Egypt, to blossom in Brazil, to fructify in Singapore.

•

I wished to see through the eyes of others. How the world looked to them. How its people appeared. How birth and death were portrayed. How gods and spirits were personified. How prayer, meditation, fasting, rituals, and rites of passage proceeded. How life happened within the familial circle. Ways in which the *why* of life was explored.

And more: the relationship of personal spirituality and institutional faiths. The perceptions of earth's population augmentation, ecological management, resource allocation. How the individual finds his or her center, feels whole and fulfilled. The metaphors for the explanation of the mystical. The connection of the universe with the mud and puddles of seasonal existence.

Were their saints? By whatever name, in whatever tradition. How did they behave? Were they respected when living? Regarded as role-models or trouble-makers? As I walked the streets of Costa Rica or Hong Kong or Johannesburg, who there had found the way to the elegant rebirth, the immaculate transformation?

•

In Nepal, on the peak of the hill outside Katmandu, the great stupa overlooked the surrounding terrain. We circumambulated the giant structure, as a Hindu-Buddhist explained this as a three-dimensional representation of the steps toward enlightenment. A visual aid for attaining nirvana. We spun prayer wheels as he laughed, "Hindu is for extroverts who need outward movement and action. Buddhist is for introverts who must turn within. They balance each other, and we are whole!"

•

In India, on the Ganges River, in the predawn darkness, from small boats, we floated lighted candles on leaf-like holders onto the water. A spangle of pilgrims' flickering prayer flames followed the current. For what did each one pray?

•

In the Peruvian Andes, with clouds catching on mountain peaks, a man of Quetchua background explained the energy of life, Wiracocha, the formless, that infused all forms with energy for their temporary existence. He displayed what he identified as a copy of an ancient drawing, with recognizable depictions of animals, plants, and humans surrounding an oval representing the force that empowered all else. He added that the understanding of this central universal energy had been misrepresented by the conquerors of his ancestors.

•

Along the teeming waters of the Amazon, we glided in a wooden flatboat up the tributaries and walked through rain forest vegetation, visiting tribal homes in the jungle interior, seeking to know their stories. A Brazilian guide said. "For this tribe, there are no stories left." Their ancestors had been coastal, and all of their interlocking tales of creation and existence had been woven into the sea and tides and boats and fishing. From these had come their metaphors and symbols. When Portuguese exploiters had arrived to harvest the riches of the interior, they had enslaved the group and forced them on what became for many a death march away from the ocean. The survivors' descendants lived now in a storiless void, where the old tales, making no sense in this alien setting, had atrophied and died to memory. He said that for an individual to make sense of a personal chronicle, it must be connected to a greater narrative of the cosmos.

•

Standing by the Shinto shrine in Japan, the Japanese business worker explained the continuity of the family through all the generations who came before. Hatsu miya-mairi, one of the cycle of life rites of Shinto practice, refers to the day when the girl-baby, on the thirty-third day after birth, and the boy on the thirty-second, is brought by its grandmother or mother to the kami and becomes acknowledged as a human being, linked with the ancestors. And what does it mean to become human?

•

Driving with a native of Bangkok through its streets at rush hour, with traffic compressed on narrow lanes in a tangle of vehicles, he smiled. "Notice how no one becomes impatient or angry. Except occasional foreigners." He smiled again. "Christian missionaries have been coming here for centuries. They find few converts. Why would anyone want to trade their peace and tranquility for sin and guilt? The little realized fact is that more of the missionaries converted to Buddhism than the other way around." He smiled again, and we drove on toward what he described as the largest restaurant in the world, covering several acres.

•

Delphi. Standing before the foundation of the oracle's temple on the mountainside, I imagined the structure still rising on the rocky slope in Greece. For a thousand years the Pythia's voices spoke Apollo's words to priests to translate for seekers. Unrecorded centuries before that, Gaia's voice informed her women priests. In my mind's eye, I could see, emblazoned still, the carved words on either side of the entry: *Know yourself. In all things, moderation.*

•

Along the road in rural India walked a naked man toward whom the few people he passed bowed and raised their palm-pressed hands. My Indian companion said, "Jain, from the Sankrit word for saint. He has literally detached himself from material belongings. He has no home, no possessions, no clothing. He seeks inner awareness and shares it with others." Another man walked several paces behind, accompanying the saint from a village he had stayed in for a few days where people had gathered around him for instruction. Someone from the next village would meet him and walk the remaining distance behind him to that locale. Again he would teach, and they would provide him meager food, and he would walk on. And so he would move through his life. "He is as free of earthly attachments as the day he was born."

•

I stood in Egypt, amid the remnants of antiquity. In one location, many of the relief carvings of the gods had their heads chiseled off, replaced with even-sided crosses. "The early Christians," explained an Egyptian, "sought to reduce the power of the other deities by beheading their representations and replacing their faces with crosses, vandalizing the ancient works."

He explained that long before Christianity, this equal-sided cross depicted the four directions, each associated with an animal, a color, and human attribute. The sides had to all be the same size, to be in harmony, and the human must make the circle of them all to be in balance and find one's center. "And we have long known," he added, "that the Roman cross was out of balance, the sides being unequal. It could not bring people using it to inner and outer harmony."

•

In Japan, China, Nepal, and India, I talked with Buddhists and Taoists. A word is but a pointing finger, they said, and must not be mistaken for the moon at which it points. A word is unimportant, except to call attention to a reality it represents. Religious edifices, stained glass, murals, statues—all are symbols, like words, like a finger, pointing. The words and symbols only have significance if they become transparent, invisible, and the viewer moves through them to the inner state of transcendence, a transcendence of the limitations of symbols.

Backstage

The odyssey continued in another unexpected way. As a university teacher in communication, requests came to serve as consultant for various business, government, health care, and educational organizations. Among them, religious institutions called. While their public exterior, like a stage, stood prepared for the audience, the denominations invited me, as a consultant, backstage, seeking intervention strategies for a variety of concerns, another source of stories.

•

The ministerial assistant said that he felt his denomination was hide-bound, lacking in respect for education and personal exploration, that it was time to open the windows and let in fresh air. He wanted to arrange a series of educational seminars for church leaders and parishioners with an outside speaker rather than himself. His denomination's attitude was that parishioners were easier to control if information came from ordained leaders and only dealt with official doctrine. He felt that this perspective was not true religion and wanted to initiate change, but if he did it himself, he would be replaced.

•

"You're a neutral observer," the small group of people from a troubled congregation said. "We have a religious problem we've got to discuss." "What about your minister?" I asked. "We can't," they responded, "the church is arguing over who's in control, and we can't take sides Our families are hurting under the stress. We need help with this, but we don't have anyone we can talk to there."

•

The men in the wood-paneled suite, to which they had invited me, sat in the plush-cushioned chairs of a board room for one of their administrative bodies, collectively representing the leadership of a range of religious organizations. These inter-faith administers, the chairperson explained, perceived a common need in that they all gave lip-service to the furtherance of interracial involvement, but in their day-by-day activities, little existed. They wanted outside help to open up their services and social activities to diversity, and to encourage their parishioners in their workplaces to do the same. "We need an outsider, so none of us are blamed by some for moving too slowly nor by others for moving too fast, who won't be bogged down in the internal politics."

•

The twenty-year-old minister in jeans and T-shirt that proclaimed I AM THE LORDS explained that he just stood up one day, after what he called a life of waste and degradation, and started preaching, and his listeners shouted, praise the Lord. He said, "I'm getting paid and having a ball. I don't know what I'm doing, but I've been called to do it. Until they stop me. Could you help me with my communication skills?"

•

The church was falling apart, said their representatives who came for consultation. Some liked the minister, others did not. The programs were too formal for some, too lax for others. There was too little emphasis on minorities for some and too much for others. Some welcomed alternative lifestyles; others did not. Some thought it was too unspiritual, others too unsocial. The membership agreed on only one thing: they wanted reexamination, weeks or months, if necessary.

The resulting intervention that I conducted included focus groups, workshops, personal journals, and meetings to evaluate the findings, identify problems, and project solutions. The congregation poured out their earnest search for meaning in their lives, trying to shape the institution to meet their needs, revealing a network of complex interrelationships, as they searched to define and achieve fulfillment together.

•

The Lutheran leader had a running joke of chiding me, in his booming voice, for my interest in race and religion, saying that every religion and race had its proper position, if they "keep their place and don't try to mix with mine." One day he telephoned. "Everything's wrong," he said, almost whispering that one of his children had "married a Jew " and another had "married a black." He wondered where had he failed as a parent. The background groups of neither couple were accepting the pairings. What was he supposed to do? What would happen to grandchildren? What would they be, and who would accept them? He had to "fix things" for them, since they would be his only heirs. Then the booming voice returned. "Come to my church next week. I'll arrange for you to speak, and you can tell them what they're supposed to do."

•

"We're extending ourselves," the minister said. "We're inviting the wicans to have an earth ceremony in our church for the equinox. This is a big step toward tolerance to have a witches' fest in our sanctuary, and some of our people are going to be upset. I want you there in case we need help communicating."

•

I coordinated monthly general systems discussions on whatever subject we might wish, with dozens of people of a variety of ages, backgrounds, interests, and occupations, to explore a range of ideas. Participants suggested topics, one of which was new age religion. I contacted a person who distributed

new age materials, inviting her to speak. "New age," she laughed,
"has been around from the beginning." She described how it was
not new in the historical sense, but a manner of looking at things,
a way of being open and inquisitive. "Some people who identify
themselves as new age get too narrow and become just as
conservative as the organizations they object to." She told the
group, "Leo Tze, Jesus, Galileo, were all new age. They saw
visions beyond the boundaries of the generally accepted and
dared to explore them." One listener said she had come prepared
to disagree but found herself included in this definition.

•

Members of a large church were divided. Their minister rented
out meeting rooms in his complex to a wide range of small groups
of other denominations who did not have their own space, as a
way to demonstrate interfaith tolerance. When one group held a
union ceremony for two men, the minister terminated the group's
access. He explained that he personally didn't mind same-gender
couples, but that his superiors disagreed, and they controlled the
budget. After all, he concluded, the church is first and foremost
an economic-based institution. You have to exist to do good, he
explained, so you don't take a stand on principles that threaten
your income.

•

The ministers of a church complex wanted an outsider to
come and conduct a workshop from an objective point of view on
their creed, a many-page document that members accepted when
they joined, as the focus of their lives. Something was lacking,
the ministers felt, but could not define exactly what. I began the
workshop with the question, how many of you have read it? The
ministers laughed and said I need not waste time for that, since
the entire congregation had studied it daily since enrollment. I
assured them this was basic to all subsequent workshop activities
and had the participants turn in unsigned written responses to

avoid the peer pressure of hand-raising. The tally showed that the same number had studied it as there were ministers but none of the rest had ever read it.

Observations

People told stories of personal experiences that became defining moments of understanding for their spiritual views.

One college teacher said, "As a child, I wondered how religion began. Then I pictured a shepherd out all day under the sky, who just knew that God was there, and right from wrong. And from then on, my religion was a reflection of that moment."

"My baby was born," said one woman, "and immediately, I knew what life was all about."

"I am a Presbyterian Buddhist," explained a teacher of comparative religion. "I discovered when I connected these two, I found my own religion."

"You've got to believe in something," explained an artist. "So I chose a church with nice activities and go there. I volunteer to teach classes and count the collections and baby sit, but never sit through a service."

A school teacher in midwest America considered that her religion was what she did daily with her eighth grade class, the way she treated them, the opportunities she opened to them. Biologically childless, she considered these as her spiritual children, and her classroom as her house of worship.

An octogenarian in Missouri expressed her concept of religion with a simple smile: "Well, it's doing what's right. Everyone knows what's right, and you just do it. You don't need all the rest. Just do what's right."

A sociology teacher felt that religious choice was predetermined by personality preferences which were inborn. "Give a student a personality inventory, and I'll tell you the kind of religion he'll migrate to and what his definition of religion will be."

•

Two people had repeated arguments about religion being good or bad, without ever fully defining the word *religion*. One said religion taught that God was a sixty-year-old white man floating in a bathrobe, zapping people, that it fostered prejudice, sexism, and wars. The second said religion saw God as a spirit, uniting people, ending conflict. The first challenged the second's views as naive, saying he was ignoring several thousand years of historical evidence. The second replied that nothing the first was talking about was religion anyway, just wrong interpretations.

•

The Japanese teacher could not stop giggling, saying that conservative American fundamentalists were so funny. They believed in water that parted, in a man born without a father inseminating the mother, in creatures with feathery wings living in the clouds, in a talking snake, in a rib becoming a woman, in pushing people under water so they would not go to a volcano pit after they died, in a bad superhuman and a good superhuman who murdered a man's wife and children in a contest to see what the man would do, in a muscleman who was strong because of long hair.

She laughed while trying to politely hide her face behind her hands. "If I told my family those things, they would think I was crazy. What do these things have to do with religion?"

•

"Some call me a witch, but I prefer pagan," the medical technician said. "The world is here, with its seasons and plants and animals. All the other stories that religious tell about revelations and rules are just so many distractions from the truth.

The truth is all around us. I celebrate the equinox and the solstice in a pure form instead of doctoring it up as Easter or Passover or the other superimposed names."

•

The native American youth working as an artist's model leaned back against the wooden pole supporting the porch overlooking a desert expanse. He said, "I tell people, if what you believe makes you treat me like yourself, then it's good. If not, it's evil. Don't talk to me of doctrine, just treat me like yourself. A family of missionaries—not Christians, but some new cult who say they're newer and better than the Christians—wanted to teach my family. I listened politely once and then told them I would watch them for a year, and if they treated everyone like themselves, I would come back to hear more."

•

"If you've got to call me something," said the African physicist, "then say I am an animist. There is a spirit to all things. And all our spirits are connected. And the more we understand those connections, the more we take care of everything, for we are inseparable from everything else. I am a scientist, and for me, to be a scientist is to be an animist. For every subatomic particle is a force relating to all other forces."

•

The medical intern explained, "My parents said that religious organizations did more harm than good, and withdrew from church membership when I was born, so I wouldn't be polluted by religio-centrism. I don't know traditions of any group, except through the popular media. If I'm not religious, what am I? My morals seem as good as anyone else's and some say I'm the most spiritual person they know."

•

In California, the artist watched me intently during our conversation. "It's bright," he said at last. "Your aura. I usually don't mention it, because people think it's strange, but I see them all the time. And yours is bright and flaming. I don't know what I'm seeing, but it's how I know about people."

•

The nun, over coffee and bagels in New England, said, "I remember how I came to understand that spiritual illumination can be obtained in many ways, including sexual contact. One of the delightful priests I suggested this to seemed surprised at first, then agreed. But he could never seem to get over his feelings of guilt at this most natural of God's gifts and simply enjoy the expansion of consciousness that the experiences brought."

•

"Some of these self-help, spiritual guide books are a rip-off, " the lady behind the counter said. She sold such volumes in her spiritually oriented shop. "They tell you things as common as when you wake up, get out of bed, and if you're hungry, eat. And you should be happy not sad. See what I mean? The obvious." She hit her forehead with the palm of her hand in a gesture of exasperation.

•

The researcher was bothered about the meditation training he had attended. "This meditation master, who lives off of donations, kept talking about how fortunate people like him were to be free of family and work and distracting responsibilities, so they could make great spiritual progress. The rest of us, who had been sucked into the life of employment and family responsibilities, could only make a little progress. But we were footing the bill for his workshop. If the spiritual path can't work for everyone, then what good is it?"

•

A minister, facing retirement, spoke of his past religious certainties fading now. "I did everything I was supposed to but went through the motions without ever finding what I expected to be there. Now I'm going back and trying some things I bypassed before because they seemed frivolous. I've always wanted to act on stage, so at last I've volunteered for the little amateur theater. Is that frivolous? I did everything in my religion that I was supposed to, and all of it now seems so empty."

•

The gentleman from Asia, now living in another continent, identified himself as a gay female-impersonator. He explained his sense of peacefulness. "As a child I received Buddhist training and saw that dualities caused sorrow. I learned how the dualities are imaginary, and with that realization, the sorrows ended. Now I live in peace, even though I am a minority within a minority within a minority. But when duality ceases, there are no minorities."

•

Pointing to the ancient terracing in the mountains in Ecuador, where his native people had maintained the land for centuries, and comparing that to the eroding hillsides where the Europeans had imposed their devastating practices, the man pronounced his Quechua word *Pachakutik*. This, he explained, came from the combined words for *earth* and *time*, referring to the concept of continuing spiritual balance of the ecological system of the land and the humans. "In true religion, we care for the land, otherwise we do not have true religion," he said.

•

The missionary had spent years in Asia. "I don't preach, ever," she said. "I only work in schools teaching world literature, where I have something real and useful to offer. If they learn anything from my life, as I live it, well and good. But I can never hold myself up as an example to anyone. Who am I to say how anyone else should believe or live their lives?"

From the Abstract
To the Behavioral

A professional academic association included a panel on religious communication in their conference and asked me to explore the underlying unity of surface-different creeds and present a paper on the results.

Approaching people of a wide spectrum of beliefs, I asked them a series of questions about what their personal goals were from their faith practices.

Among their responses: Salvation, holiness, enlightenment, insight, nirvana, illumination, social order, freedom from sin, beatitude, harmony, atonement, merging with the cosmos, following the prophet, living the scriptures, Buddha mind, walking in God's path, upliftment, finding the kingdom within, providence, inspiration, hearing the still small voice, doing right, loving all humanity, bringing the kingdom of God on earth, living in harmony with all life, saving the world, following the laws of God, preparing for heaven, eliminating duality, satori, becoming a Bodtisatva, understanding karma, doing right by others, being spiritual, becoming an angel, being a soldier for God, being at peace, using a mantra, following the Tao, grace, reaching epiphany, tariki, meditating to the point of non-words, increasing spirituality, doing good works, living a good life, experiencing communion, hearing the ancestors' guidance, honoring the previous generations, upholding the true traditions, setting the standard, living each day as if it is all of life.

I took the key words most important to their goals and asked them individually to go from a high abstraction, like *salvation*, down to behavioral terms, describing specific actions toward others. At first, many were stuck in word repetitions. *Salvation, you know, salvation, you have to have salvation.* So I would ask, how does that affect you in getting up in the morning, eating breakfast, choosing clothing to wear, and selecting films to see?

The pathway from the abstraction—what does *holy* mean to you and how do you know when you see *holy* in action—to behavioral terms proved frequently frustrating to them. Trying to explain *holy* in relation to television sitcoms and food choices required effort. The farther we proceeded, the more behavioral examples emerged, resulting in moments of discovery. Hearing themselves struggle to relate *salvation* and a tennis game could bring an exclamation of *now I understand!*

The closer we came to behavioral descriptions, the more alike the individuals' goals sounded. The views of a Kenyan animist, freed from specific worldview-bound terminology, prompted an orthodox minister to say, *Yes, that's what I meant.* When a Hindu student distilled his abstractions into behavioral terms, a Baptist engineer could respond, That's what I intended.

Gathering a variety of these people into the same room for discussion brought different results before and after the exercises. Before the abstractions had been translated into action terms, the participants saw each other as different, and the terms became cultural, semantic barriers. Later, when I could read to them a distilled collection of their activity goals dealing with desirable behaviors, freed from group-specific jargon, they each tended to claim the descriptions as their own, often surprised that the others did also. A Tibetan monk after speaking about *Buddha mind* and an Episcopal priest describing *grace* could conclude that they were really talking about the same thing, and embrace each other.

So, if you seek to be *holy*, do you play basketball? If you wish *salvation*, do you eat hot dogs? Is there a way to plan a family vacation and conduct it that is different for the person who wishes *satori* and one who does not? How does a person talk to the janitor, the billionaire, the shaman, the child, if one seeks to be *reborn* or yearns for *illumination*?

What Were We Looking For?

On that summer day in a small town, local members of a newer religious organization, most of them converts, discussed what were we looking for when we joined the group? As the hot afternoon wore on, to the drone of the flies and the unsuccessful window air conditioner, the believers shared their conversion memories.

They each had come to a point in their lives when they wondered *why* about the world's problems, about their own loneliness and imperfect relationships. They wanted someone, some external authority, to provide the answers. Then one day—that was how many began their conversion stories—they met someone in a park, airport, or at work, who mentioned that they, too, had wondered, prayed for guidance, and had found this new group. When the seekers had expressed interest, the already-believer had invited them to meetings and offered apparent friendship. They began to feel wanted in a community with a round of continuous activities. Their transfer of allegiance often came at period involving some break with their past, when they had been ripe for the something different than what they had known.

I heard similar stories, in different contexts, in many parts of the world, of people leaving familiar conditions inherited from other people. Common phrases described their new group: They *found a family*. They realized they had *always been one of this new group*, but didn't know it *until they met them*.

•

I listened to a once-student from the mid United States who took a global back-packing trip to *find himself* after what he called the routine, boring, confinement of college, before entering the routine, boring, confinement of a job. Hiking across India, he stopped in an ashram hospice for a night's cheap dwelling. After a meager meal, he joined in the evening discussion and stayed for twenty years, intending to stay forever. His phrases: I found my real family. My traditional religious background didn't satisfy. Here I was set free.

As I traveled across India a short distance from the ashram where the North American's two-decade overnight stay was occurring, I talked with another man, native to India, of similar age to the American. This individual had been raised from childhood in the spiritual procedures which had entranced the former back-packing student. I asked this man born in India of his practices—meditation, exploration of the spiritual in an ashram? He informed me that he wanted to travel to a location in America, relatively close to the place the former student had come from, where the Hindu felt he could really begin to live, instead of being stifled, going nowhere, being tradition bound. These two people, unknown to each other, wanted, in effect, to trade places, and for much the same reasons.

•

The mountaineer oriented everything—his job, family, finances—to climb. Work, save funds, climb. Always farther and higher. We sat in a desert-region shelter, from which he planned his next foray, as he described the confines of the business that fed his bank account. When the financial thermostat hit a certain level, he took extended leaves, evacuated the claustrophobic confines of the city, and sped into the wilderness to leap crevasses and pull himself up cliff faces. Why? To escape the dreary routine. To be with his family of climbers who, like him, were not tamed by urban living. He felt closer to the answers to life on mountain tops.

•

The family from the plains states had fled dirt farming to give their lives to the Lord in what they called the ultimate sacrifice, leaving their country to head into the wilderness of a foreign land to bring the redeeming message to the heathen. They adopted native children who the Lord had put into their keeping, children who were intended to grow in the spiritual light and share it with their own people. I talked with the couple as they recounted the rich lives they now led in their missionary outpost, with their greatest works being their native children.

At a later time, I met with those native children, apart from their adoptive parents, sent from the jungle to the heartland of the United States, to a denominational school for proper training. They said their adoptive parents, while well meaning, lived lives that were tedious and ineffective. The children wanted to escape that and live in California where real life existed and find themselves and the fulfillment they sought.

•

The self-defined former cult member described how years earlier he had been a solitary seeker who wanted to find spiritual salvation for everyone. His home church, family, schools, and government, had, in his estimation, made the social mess around him. He prayed for answers and found a cult that seemed to provide them. He cut off communication with his parents and immersed himself in his new family, who promised solutions to everything, if only the faithful did what their particular divine messenger told them to do. In time, the old suffocation he had left surrounded his new routine as well, as his new messiah turned out to be a machinator. So the seeker had escaped, and, still loving what he had first thought the cult was, but turned out not to be, he now searched for that vision in some new form.

•

I conducted a seminar on creativity, where a soft-spoken participant explained to the group how she had attempted suicide. She had found her family, friends, church, and social circles inadequate and void of insight. Instead of seeking out a new geographical location, a new organization, a new ashram, a new mountain top, she chose to try to leave this life altogether and enter a new existence. She had felt that whatever came after this life had to be better than what she had experienced.

•

The sun was rolling around the horizon in perpetual twenty-four hour summer light when I spoke on a university campus in Finland. A local professor explained that many felt blessed to live in a land so economically sound, so educationally based. But why, she mused, are there so many suicides, especially men? What more could they be looking for?

•

A whole band of restless individuals had felt stifled by their backgrounds. The routine, the familiar, the scramble for the loot of materialism, sent them all delving into unexplored alternatives. They found each other and banded into a migrant commune that wandered together seeking their promised land.

Their members told me the story. The breaking of former ties to search for the unknown fulfillment, the bonding with the new family of traveling companions. Different, daring, adventurous, they finally found their private land of milk and honey, settled, rooted, built a new community for themselves. They fenced in their compound and in time became wealthy.

The children, the second generation, born in the promised land, inside those fences, came separately to tell me more. One said, "My parents think this is such a big deal. They broke with their traditions and set up a new way of life. But that was their life. I was raised in it. What's so great about it? How is it really different? There has got to be something for me. I've got to break loose and find it. They say, we already did that. For them, maybe. They just don't understand."

•

Some are discontent with the routine of the familiar and seek the new family, the authoritative answers from another source. They become vulnerable to self-serving groups touting divine world orders and revelations, if they do not separate what is merely new and seemingly authoritative from what is redemption defined in behavior.

Perspectives

Some people I spoke with emphasized repetitions of activities, while others emphasized the desire for variety.

"We must create some more rituals for the holiday," said a business manager. For her, life was a series of repeated patterns, building a set of repetitions for her family, for every birthday, holiday, and the private celebrations. What did she seek? Nothing. Life, for her, became a series of short dramatic scripts, acted out over and over again. She even had a scenario planned for the birthdays when behavior would change after each decade.

In contrast, a student's story revealed that she had backpacked across the country and across two other continents. Her available time found her in groups helping race relations, women's rights, sexual orientation groups, sweat lodge retreats, mountain hikes that ending in the capital rotunda speaking against clear-cutting policies. "I keep looking," she said, "and I know so little." Her routines and rituals? Virtually nonexistent. No repeated celebrations. To do it once meant to bypass it a second time. She migrated through experiences, avoiding repetitions.

•

Others' perspectives were influenced in contrasting ways by focusing more either on the concrete or on the general. With the first, a person can shop, give directions, and plan schedules, while with the second, one can spread imaginative canopies to cover the gaps of experiences. Moving from one to the other can bring a change of perspective.

A student who had been focusing on life as a series of specific details, suddenly saw it as a whole, with results that startled her. The youth, unconsciously pendulumed her long hair behind her back, said in perplexity, "Why should I complete an education and look for a job, or even eat breakfast, when I'm going to die?" Soon? Not necessarily. Just that she felt stranded in a new awareness that life leads to death. Always. And in that context, why study, why work, why eat, why do anything?

•

A twenty-five-year-old sucked his lips for a moment, making a decision. He plunged in, breathing deeply. "I was twenty-one and bullet proof. I only saw the moment I was living in." He could not sit still. "I was going to live forever. I was eternal." He paced. "Then I had these strange symptoms and checked with a doctor." He spoke the polysyllabic Latin medical terms of the diagnosis and prognosis. Pulling up his shirt, he revealed a scar from thorax to abdomen, saying he may be dead by thirty and that had changed his perspective on everything.

•

The former television newscaster made imaginary lines toward the ceiling with his index fingers. "In the beginning that has no beginning, God loved our creation so extensively, that he made it come into being, and it will exist until the end that has no end." He now traveled and spoke for his religious organization, using phrases such as this. After the disappointment of the cancellation of his television contract, he met a true believer, who showed him the right path, and he had been showing it to others ever since, expenses paid. Religion for him became the beginningless beginning and the endless end, and a deity who loved an uncreated creation and then created it. When asked what those abstract phrases meant, the recycled newscaster said, "It is clear to those who understand and unclear to those who do not."

•

At the ninety-five-year-old lady's wake, another nonagenarian stood at the casket patting the deceased's newly waved, blue-silver hair. I heard her say to those clustered around, "Oh, such a lovely permanent, the best she's ever had!" They conversed about the specifics of the beautiful hair, each touching it and describing its excellence. The minister, at the funeral, spoke abstractly of her heavenly home and place in eternity, but he said not a word about the specifics of her postmortem permanent.

•

The religion professor questioned why artists' beatific renderings only show Jesus cradling sheep or holding a child on his lap. Where are the paintings of Jesus changing a baby's diapers or wiping off the result of the sheep defecating on him?

He also speculated on what the following answers conveyed about the perspective of two construction workers to the question, "What are you doing?" The first, "Putting one stone on top of another." The second, "I'm building a cathedral."

He also raised the question of why the songs of religious groups sing praises of abstractions like amazing grace, glory, and redemption but never praise the virtue of specifics like meatloaf or vacuuming.

Franchising Reality

Many that I spoke with felt there was a major distinction between worldviews that people practiced for their own development, and those that people insisted were the one right way and sought to impose on others. Some said the latter appeared to be an attempt to franchise *reality* by implying that the only valid approach to understanding existence came through the channels of their founder and organization.

•

In public meetings, members of one *true faith* proclaimed its total acceptance of all other religions, luring those who appreciated ecumenism. But subsequent indoctrination emphasized that the other faiths had been right only in their own time and place. Now this one superseded them all, the only valid way to God at this time in history, the only one that could explain what the others, now hopelessly corrupted, really meant.

•

"Why must we all believe in your messenger as the only right way to God?" the asker questioned at the public lecture for another of the new organizations. The speaker responded, "if God revealed his full glory, humans couldn't stand it." The visitor said, "But God could make everyone able to withstand this full glory." "That's not the way he did it," said the speaker loudly, "so he had to select one special channel who could withstand the full glory, and the rest of us must believe unquestioningly in that one channel as the only manifest word of God for centuries to come."

·

I asked a believer in one of the new faiths about the non-traditional calendar on the wall. She said, "When God speaks to mankind again, we cannot keep dates in the old way. Our new prophet revealed this new calendar dating from the year his ministry began, with new holy days commemorating his life, and new month names." Asked if she was familiar with the many calendars of other groups, she said, "Those are false calendars since this is the only one God uses now."

·

Members of one *ultimate religion* described an administrator who had demanded obedience from the faithful, admonishing those accused of disobedience in scathing epistles and summoning them before the tribunal. Presiding over its social executions and character assassinations, he aimed a pointing finger, reminding them that this was the institution of God speaking. Then word came forth from their headquarters, in just such a character-depreciating message about him. Speculation spread of infighting between two factions, seeking control of the religion's resources. Some now saw the organization as inherently flawed, as factions vied internally for a greater market share of their attempt to franchise reality.

·

The *true faith* speaker described with flair an episode in his group's history. "The enemies rushed into the house where the faithful disciples were meeting. Suddenly there was an earthquake, the wrath of God manifest. The building crumbled to dust, killing the attackers of the faith, safeguarding the believers from the hands of the enemy!" When questioned, it turned out that the faithful all died in the same way. But "they were taken to the heavenly folds, to inspire forever the souls of man throughout this dispensation." The same demise with two distinctly different interpretations.

•

"Official versions of religious history do it all the time," said a historian, "putting their interpretation as fact, and underplaying or omitting contrary views. We hear of Christians being fed to the lions in Roman arenas, but how many preach about what happened after Christianity became the official religion of Rome? The arena killings continued without interruption as the Christians fed non-Christians to the lions, and onlookers cheered in the name of Jesus."

•

The business man asked what to do about his religion which had censured researchers who claimed the founder was a human, subject to development and change. The administration insisted that their prophet was infallible and unchanging from the moment he received his revelation. They locked away accessibility of archival material to people who researched history in the academic way, appointing their own officially approved writers, who would begin with the premise of perfection and infallibility. "How does this differ from any other dictatorship?" he asked.

•

Prophecies from many groups were generalized mixes of symbols and numbers similar to: *Bears and eagles will clash. When one has become three, the lightning will strike. The great will fall and the fallen shall become enlarged. The wall will become the bridge when the vision has appeared.* These would then be connected to actual dates, locations, and people by later official interpreters, recited by the devout as evidence of the founder's superhuman powers.

"Fortune cookies," said one observer, "like reading today *you will go somewhere, and tomorrow you will meet someone.* And, of course, you do, and after the fact, can attach the names of those real people and places. It's only proof of our gullibility."

•

A believer in a recent religious founder declared his leader's infallibility to his audience. When one listener asked for evidence of this claim, the speaker said, "Because God told him he was infallible. And he told us. And God cannot be wrong."

•

A member of a new religious community said to non-members over dinner, "You must enter the true religion," referring to his own. Asked if this was a social conversation or part of a report to his organization, he stammered, gesturing broadly as if to push away the question, splashing coffee in the process. He insisted that this was the only truth of God for this age. Their plan was to establish a theocracy, rejoining church and state, with his church to become everyone's state, the world government, their version of the kingdom of God on earth.

•

A religionist from the Near East with a reputation for benevolence, held a high position in his recently developed religion. But when asked about some researched materials that indicated his prophet-founder had multiple spouses, the apparent benevolence changed. In an emotional display, he demanded silence about the fact that his prophet practiced and taught polygamy. Especially since the official brochures currently touted monogamy.

•

One religious organization, promoting its public image as a champion of human rights, presented awards to those outside their membership who had furthered this goal. I was invited to meet with their selection committee to offer recommendations for nominees. As suggestions were made, the panel disregarded their human rights achievements and evaluated them only by the publicity they would generate and their name draw to bring out a crowd to the ceremony which, it turned out, fronted as a way to proselytize to an unsuspecting audience. When I questioned the difference between their stated intentions and their actual purpose, one said, *we have to spread the true word of God any way we can.*

•

A researcher received a letter from the administration of one of the recent religions claiming to be the only valid update of God's word. Publicly, they pointed proudly to such innovations as banning book destruction and promoting the unrestricted search of truth. They had heard that he had recently obtained an out-of-print volume that included unauthorized translations of what they considered to be their *scriptures.* They told him not to read the book and to send it to them immediately, so their *spiritual institution* could dispose of it properly. Yet they publicly continued to proclaim that they banned book destruction and promoted unrestricted search for truth.

•

If older scriptures of various faiths referred to a time when *the power of God will shine forth, or the greatness of the Lord will appear,* then the founders of newer groups may take these designations for themselves, replacing their birth names with titles such as *God's Greatness,* or the *Power of God,* in whatever language they were speaking. Then the followers could teach that the holy books of the past predicted his coming, foretelling his exact name. A speaker from a modern group started by such a self-renamed founder said, "No one can doubt such specific references. This is absolute evidence that former prophets foretold the coming of our prophet."

•

A man spoke rhapsodically about his new religion including such God-directed innovations as not having paid clerics, who could be corrupted by their positions. Instead, in his faith, dedicated administrators, like himself, took care of affairs. He said he lived on only a modest expense account to help carry out God's work. When his coworker discussed their extensive travel, she described how they stayed only at *the finest high-class hotels.* "After all," she said, "our members are the only ones doing the true work of the Lord and have to represent God properly."

•

Followers of the *true faith* may claim it can never be divided. The appearance of offshoots and splinter groups may be dismissed as personal ego trips of small-minded people who will soon be forgotten. "How otherwise could God demonstrate the strength of his cause if it was never challenged?" rhetorically questioned a speaker on *a new way to God,* who refused to acknowledge the existence of factions.

•

To a speaker who had converted to the *only true faith,* a man from the audience asked how she explained that her group appeared to be a money machine, urging the faithful to sacrifice to support the administrators. She pointed out that believers will always be reimbursed by God, so there is no sacrifice. "God will not be in debt to anyone who supports the only true faith."

•

I walked out of a store in another country and saw *the look.* Something about this stranger in the crowd seemed familiar, having seen others with a similar look before, spreading *the true cause of God.* She was the *teacher,* the *proselytizer,* the *missionary,* the *settler,* the *deputy for God,* by whatever name they were called. She had the body posture, the gestures, the look cast at faces of passersby, trying to single out the one who makes eye contact, the one who looks ready for *the message.*

I made eye contact. Her pupils dilated. She brushed her sleeve back, glancing at her empty arm. "Do you have the time?" I told her the hour and minutes.

"Oh, the weather," she said, "isn't it charming? How God has blessed us with days like this. Don't you agree?" Gazing skyward, she said, "Oh, look!" as if someone were descending. "What?" I asked.

"You see," she said, her voice dreamy. "We rush so much, don't we, in our materialistic culture, that we miss..." She was groping now. "...the sky!" She waved her hands in a general upward direction and giggled slightly, assuming a *pieta* look as she stared directly into my eyes. "Oh, I can see you are one who *does* watch the sky. You have such a spiritual feeling about you. Oh, isn't that wonderful."

Inwardly, I tried to predict the coming sequence: sky to *spiritual* to *messenger of God for this day*, while she moves me from the pedestrian stream. "I'm just overjoyed, myself, to be living in this day of God! And to have recognized him, in this, his new garb." She gave a practiced laugh, as if at her own childlike enthusiasm while directing me out of the pedestrian traffic. "Oh, you may not know what I'm talking about, although..." Another madonna expression. "...I think you do. You do feel the tug of the new age dawning. A new messenger of God has appeared and revealed all the solutions. Redemption is at hand!"

I predicted inwardly: transition to personal life, not from here, sounds midwestern American, found the group, converted, wanted to travel, became a pilgrim for the almighty testifying for him, left her job and material belongings, a family that doesn't see the light of the new day, has limited resources, but ecstatically happy doing the will of God with her new spiritual family.

"For you see, I was once wayward and uncaring, but I found the messenger for this day. I had a really good business job in Ohio when..." And the story proceeded on track.

I continued inwardly projecting: there just happens to be a little *circle meeting* this evening in one of the local believer's homes where we can share this life-changing revelation. She continued on cue and, at the meeting part, suddenly discovered to her apparent surprise that she had small printed maps of how to get there. She emphasized that her group never proselytizes, as other groups do, but just shares the message with the receptive. Her eyes were now darting to the people walking near us, ready to move on to the next eye-contactor at the edge of the herd.

•

A member described how it seemed increasingly to him that the administrators of his *one true faith* were creating a *holy upper class*. With their authority came the final say over the allocation of scarce resources. In his view, the inner circle elite, in the guise of fellow believers doing the humble bidding of God, were building houses, offices, and providing other accommodations that the rich and powerful have controlled in other societies. He began to view his religion as an economic hierarchy—king and subject, owner and slave—with infighting for control. An organization that determined who gives commands and who carries them out and how to maintain authority in the attempt to franchise reality under the logo of the only true faith, merchandising spirituality like a product for which God had given them the exclusive patent. "Maybe I'm learning the lesson God wanted me to learn," he said, "to leave them."

Blending

She balanced on one foot, quivering a bit, and pronounced the task an outer example of inner centering. She practiced yoga and spoke of the yoking of mind, body, and spirit. She lifted a non-existent flame in her right hand, and the moon in her left, and gesturally merged them at her heart level. In and out she breathed, explaining between breaths the merging of dualities into a single whole.

"I'm Jewish," she explained, "and had some concerns—my rabbi had more—about how yoga fit into my traditions." But her background in the Kabbalah mentally merged with the body centers of yoga. The two, for her, became inseparable blended.

•

The interdenominational group discussed the basics of religion. One participant proclaimed that the Ten Commandments should be posted on the wall of every classroom in the world. When the question arose as to which version of the Ten Commandments, some were surprised to learn of the variations.

"All the versions came from Hammurabi," a professor of comparative religion stated emphatically. "He lived in eighteenth century B.C.E. Babylon and left the first major code of laws, and that was the source of the Ten Commandments at a later time." Someone protested, saying God revealed the laws to Moses. "If he did," said the professor, "they were secondhand, since Hammurabi had them first."

•

The Catholic priest motioned his flock to be seated under the branches of an oak tree. He then began his classes on Buddhism. "What Buddha taught is the heart of the Christian mystery," he said, "and what Christ sacrificed himself for, that we could discover the inner mystery, not superimpose it from outside. Buddha guides us there."

•

"The medicine wheel," said the native American woman moving her arms in a great circle, "is the invitation to enter the mystery of discovery of yourself. It conflicts with no religion, but enriches them all." A listener asked, "Including Baptist, Catholic, and Jehovah Witnesses?" "Yes," she smiled.

•

The religious group described itself as *inclusive*. At a meeting, the choir began to sing *what a friend we have in Jesus*. They continued with verses celebrating *what a friend we have in Socrates*, and continued with Confucius, Martin Luther King, Darwin, and Einstein.

•

He stretched his portly frame and chided himself, "Over fed, under exercised, smoke, drink too much, sleep deprivation—but I'm a doctor!" The physician laughed. "So, let's see, what's my religion?" He described his childhood in a Methodist family. Nuns at a nearby school welcomed this child who loved their rosaries and affection, and he converted to Catholicism. Traveling west, he campfired with a visionary who introduced them to the order of Osiris, and the youth merged into the ancient mystery tradition, until he met the woman he wedded, converting to her Judaism. When that faded, he wandered west again and lived with a Zuni family and adopted *the earth way* as his own. In the Far East, he studied the eightfold path of inner realization straight into Buddhism. During a hospital stay, he found himself under the care of a *master religionist* and steeped himself in everything written by Krishnamurti. Meeting a Universalist, he rejoiced in the salvation of everyone. He worked with a nurse imported from the British Isles whose devoutness brought him into the Church of England. A new colleague from India was currently teaching him of reincarnation, and the doctor said he could do better in his next life.

•

The writer described a colleague who would not join any organized, named tradition. "He is a secular saint. He lives a more sanctified life than anyone else I know, defining integrity by his actions. He is the most religious man I have ever met." He repeated, "A saint, a secular saint, without a church. Yet all churches are within him. He has blended the best of them all into his own private worship in daily life."

•

The lady in her lose clothing winced in front of her listeners. "Can't get into the lotus position ever again," she explained. "My doctor forbids it. Says it has ruined my knee." She eased herself, with the good leg bent, into a half lotus. She touched her midsection with her clasped fingers. "In some eastern traditions, the search for authority is from within oneself. It's already there, waiting to be discovered. Often in the west, people turn outward, wanting some paternalistic figure to come and tell them what to do. When I explored the mystics of all faiths, I realized a great truth that they are neither eastern or western. They rose above their cultures and blended."

Inside and Outside the Circles

On the opening class meeting for the semester of my university course in Intercultural Communication, I carried in the life-size stand-up figure of a not-from-earth character from a science fiction cinema series and stood it in the middle of the room. "Imagine," I told the students, "that there is a circle on the floor around the base of our intergalactic visitor. He stands inside. All who are *non-he* remain outside. Much cultural study is based on this simple example. Every group, when it is named, gains a semantic circle around it. The study of culture attributes names to projected differences for those inside the circle and those outside of it."

Religion influences where we draw those lines and how we respond to those perceived differences.

•

He served as a minister in a United States *relocation camp*. I sat in his living room discussing his memories. He recalled how those in America of Japanese ancestry were forcibly removed from their properties and imprisoned during the Second World War, after President Roosevelt signed Executive Order 9066 on February 19, 1942. He spoke of the tragedy of the whole circumstance, the unfairness of it all, and of his sense of powerlessness to do anything about it.

He went further back in history. How in 1790, the national Congress had limited American citizenship to what they designated as *free white immigrants*, leaving all others, including the Japanese, outside of the citizenship circle. In California, from where many had been removed to the camps in other parts of the country, the Alien Land Law in 1913 had prevented them from even owning land.

The minister spoke of his perplexity in seeing these people he served as fellow Americans being restricted by civil authority that made them prisoners in their own land, without recourse to the justice system, with no apparent outcry from the organized religious communities, including his own.

He recalled how the Arkansas legislature, a state where two such camps were located, passed a law, as soon as the war ended, preventing those of Japanese ancestry from even buying property in the state, presumably from fear that the released prisoners would want to stay in their land of exile. He mused that it all seemed a very unreligious thing to do.

•

The soldier had been a member of a peace-keeping force in a civil-war-torn country. Chilling, he said, furrowing his brow at the memory. He described how two ethnic factions fought. How he had talked with a leader of one of the groups that had undertaken ethnic cleansing of the others outside of his circle. How the man had said with utter calmness that his people were kind and did not rape nor torture the others, they just removed them as they would any infestation of pests that plague the land. By exterminating them. The soldier asked, "How can we get them to see the others as human beings?"

•

The athlete came as guest speaker to a class I taught on communication in organizations. He had helped to operate an outreach center for those in need. "I am a human being seeking to give and receive the same compassion as others," he explained. He glanced down momentarily, then back up, telling us that he was HIV positive. For that statement, in the many contexts when he had uttered it, some people had drawn circles around him. Family, acquaintances, work associates reacted in varied ways, including those who now saw him as somehow tainted and separated from them. ""It hurts," he said, "to be responded to as a disease in human form, rather than as a human with one of many human conditions."

•

She was the picture of joviality, volunteering time from a busy work schedule to guide any group asking her aid through workshops of diversity training. She told the story of what motivated her. In high school in Georgia, several students had invited their school class to a swimming party at their parents' private club. Amid the frivolity, one friend told her to enjoy the place while she could, since her Jewish family couldn't be members. She had walked away from the laughter, separate, suddenly alone. She pictured herself in a imaginary procession of African-Americans who could not go there, of women kept from men's jobs, and of same-gender couples kept from normal acceptance. She looked at me through tears. "People are good," she said softly, "if only they can find the goodness within themselves." She held grudges against no one. Only against the circles they drew because of their flawed beliefs, and those lines she sought to erase in her series of never-ending sessions.

•

The diversity trainer described herself as *standing tall, imposingly statured, African-American, and extroverted.* In her workshop, she emphasized that if you react to someone who has marginalized you and in retaliation do the same, the result is merely a contest of who wins this round rather than a change of viewpoint. These observations followed the ganging up by those she pointed out as *the women, African-Americans, Indians, Asians, same-gender oriented, and other minorities* in her audience against the participants who were, as she described them, *white, male, straight, generically Christian-ish.*

She put her arms around the shoulders of two of the latter and said, *We have to preserve our white boys, now. Don't be jumping on them.* She explained how this same response occurred in her seminars with increasing frequency. Well-meaning persons of this category caught the flack from people of other backgrounds as the blame-it-alls for the ills of society. "These boys never owned slaves," she said, "didn't run concentration camps, didn't bash gays, never put you women out of work." She abruptly turned to them, mockingly wide-eyed, and asked, "Did you? No, they're here because they want to help, and you're doing to them what other people who may have resembled them, did to you or your ancestors. And if you don't see what you're doing, you'll perpetuate the same abuses into the future." And she hugged them both. "Momma's going to protect you," she said.

When we talked afterward, she explained that while she jokes about it during her workshop, she wants her participants to wake up to the fact that it's not categories of people who cause problems but the process of classification used. She grinned, adding, "And nobody better mess with my white boys, because they're good people."

•

Laws, policies, and practices that determine who can vote, own land, be a citizen, or continue living, are all outcomes of the worldviews of the ordinance-makers. We can search the ground around us, to see who has drawn lines encircling us and why, or if we have drawn lines around ourselves or others. Beyond that, we see the lines drawn around tundra and rain forests and deserts and lakes, around species of animals and plants, determining which to nurture and which to destroy. Within the questions of *how* and *why* those circles are drawn resides a focal point of religion.

A Gathering of Worldviews

A letter came to my university office asking me to address the subject of promoting positive interfaith discussions at a conference to which people from religious groups around the world were invited. The gathering brought together diverse participants, arrays of booths attended by members sharing their perspectives, and hundreds of presentations and panel discussions.

Participants included robed, turbaned, gowned, bejeweled, and uniformed practitioners from the reaches of the earth. The saffron-robed monk with prayer beads dangling from moving fingers mixed with variously suited people addressed as *his holiness* who were followed by entourages of briefcase-carrying assistants. Representatives argued about the protocol of seating arrangements, while near them two people who spoke no common language held hands and murmured blessings toward each other, looking through moist eyes.

In the auditorium, beneath sparkling chandeliers, the variety of garments, headgear, and emblems resembled a plumage display of a myriad avian species. A global planner warned the international assemblage from the varied religious backgrounds that if they did not cooperate actively and quickly, the earth would die of pollution and overpopulation. There were those who refused to come in, picketing outside, proclaiming that such a gathering of infidels heralded the *last days*.

•

At this conference, I presented a paper, *A Religious Subsystem Preference Inventory to Facilitate Group Discussion*, dealing with a means of promoting self-awareness about religious preferences and positive group interaction. If people talking about religion can share information rather than defending positions and trying to persuade others, greater understanding can result.

By developing pairs of opposite choices, individuals can determine which pole their preference tends toward. For example, if some people see religious activity as a group interaction while others see it as individual development, we can put these choices in two paired statements.

1A. Religion is group activity
1B. Religion is solitary.

In a discussion, participants can say which direction they prefer and briefly explain why. The choice may be seen along the line of a continuum so that a person can describe the degree of preference for either or both of the choices. In this way the participants will hear each others' viewpoints and reasons without attempting to defend or persuade.

To prepare such a list, I wanted input from people from a wide spectrum of perspectives. The one hundred and forty people participating in the survey and interviews identified their own religious-worldview perspectives in the following terms:

Agnostic, Aikidoist, anti-organized religion, Aristotelian, Assembly of God, Atheist, "balancist," Baptist, Bible-believing, Buddhist, Charismatic, Church of Christ, Christiadelfian, Christian-Republican, Conservative, Deist, Eastern Rite, eclectic, Emersonian, Environmentalist, Episcopalian, Ethicist, Existentialist, Feminist, forever seeking knowledge, Freewill Baptist, God-controlled world-view,

Goddess-worshipping, Hebrew, Hindu, Humanist, idealistic, independent philosopher, Intellectualism, Islam, Jehovah's Witness, Jewish, Joseph Campbell, Judaism, Krishnamurti, Liberal, Lutheran, Luddite, My Self, Methodist, Missionary Baptist, Monotheistic, Mormon, Mystic, Native American religion, naturalist, nature, nature mystic, Nazarene, Neo-Jungian, New Age, Non-church, Non-Teleologist, One Body of Christ Church, Pagan, Pantheist, Pentecostal, Platonist, Presbyterian, Protestant Nondenominational, Pantheistic-Reincarnation, Quaker, Quasi-spiritualist, Rationalist, Realist, Republican Fundamentalist, Researcher, Roman Catholic, science, searcher, Sentient Being, Southern Baptist, Spinoza's teachings, spiritualist, total non-conformist, Thoreauist, Twelve-Step Program, unconditional love, unique individual spirituality, Unitarian-Universalist, unnamed belief in a higher being and order and stability in the universe, World environmentalist, Zen.

On the survey form, I asked these participants to list as many subsystems as they wished that comprised their concept of religion or worldview. They listed more than one thousand items, which I categorized and then arranged in pairs of opposites.

Individuals going through the items can develop their personal profile of religion-related preferences. The directions for a group using the Inventory would be to sit in a circle, read one pair of choices, and let each person, in turn, identify his or her choice or a variation of it, or alternative, explaining briefly why, until all had expressed themselves. They could continue, in turn, with each of the other items. Participants would be asked not to make judgmental comments about each others' preferences, but to ask questions for clarity and understanding of information.

Inventory Items

1A. Religion is group activity.
1B. Religion is solitary.

2A. There is only one right religion.
2B. All religions are appropriate for the people who believe them.

3A. Only those have a religion who have membership in an organization.
3B. People's explanation of existence is their religion, even without an organization.

4A. God has an adult male form and literally exists in an actual place.
4B. God is a literary personification of some power humans feel.

5A. Religion comes from outside of human beings.
5B. Religion comes from insights within human beings.

6A. Religion needs organized leadership.
6B. Religion needs to be free of organized leadership.

7A. Religious rules should be followed whether understood or not.
7B. Religious rules can only be followed when understood and agreed with.

8A. Religious authority should never be questioned.
8B. Religious authority should always be questioned.

9A. Religious leaders should have the right to exclude or expel anyone they wish.
9B. Religious leaders should not be able to exclude anyone from membership.

10A. Religion is primarily a preparation for an after-death existence.
10B. Religion is primarily a matter of life here and now before death.

11A. My religious leadership is infallible and rules by divine right.
11B. My religious leadership is as fallible as in other organizations.

12A. Religion is a means of economic control over limited resources.
12B. Religion has little or nothing to do with economics.

13A. My religious leaders should be the civil government, joining church and state.
13B. Religious bodies and civil governments should be totally separate.

14A. I rely on my religious leaders to think and make decisions for me.
14B. I think for myself and make my own decisions.

15A. If I disagree with my religious leaders, they are right.
15B. If I disagree with my religious leaders, I am right.

16A. Religious leaders have the right to tax or tithe their members any amount.
16B. Individuals should decide if, when, and how much to contribute to religions.

17A. Belief is under my complete control; I can make myself believe.
17B. Belief is not under my control; I may want to believe but cannot will it.

18A. True religion is unchanging and always the same.
18B. True religion evolves with changing circumstances.

19A. Truth is revealed only to one or a few select humans whom others must obey.
19B. Truth is equally available to all humans, not requiring a chosen revelator.

20A. Truth is contained in a holy book, completely accurate in every detail.
20B. "Holy books" are historical, mythical, literary works of human perspectives.

21A. It is acceptable to discriminate against people of other faiths.
21B. One should behave similarly toward people within and outside of one's faith.

22A. My faith has more "good" people than other faiths.
22B. "Good" and "bad" people are found in most faiths in the same ratios.

23A. If everyone in the world joined my faith, there would be world peace.
23B. If everyone joined my faith, there would be the same problems as now.

24A. Religions prevent wars.
24B. Religions cause wars.

25A. Religions should deal with social issues.
25B. Religions should not deal with social issues.

26A. Religion frees people from prejudices such as race, gender, class, and age.
26B. Religion encourages and perpetuates those prejudices.

27A. Humans are born "sinful."
27B. Humans are born "good."

28A. Religion is primarily a matter of feeling.
28B. Religion is primarily concerned with ideas and thinking.

29A. Music and dance are important aspects of religion.
29B. Music and dance are distractions from religion, not a part of them.

30A. My religious beliefs greatly influence my daily behavior.
30B. My religious beliefs have little to do with my daily behavior.

31A. In my religion, men and women can serve in all capacities without exception.
31B. In my religion, women or men cannot serve in all capacities.

32A. Religious activities are the main source of my social life.
32B. Religious activities are secondary to my social life.

33A. It is my responsibility to try to convert others to my way of belief.
33B. I do not try to convert others.

34A. I follow religious directives from a sense of obligation and fear of punishment.
34B. I follow religious directives because of the pleasure and happiness experienced.

35A. People should marry those of the same religion.
35B. People should marry individuals of any background they wish.

36A. My religion categorizes people and tells me how to react to the categories.
36B. My religion teaches me to react to each person as an individual.

37A. Rituals are important to me.
37B. Rituals are not important to me.

38A. Art representing the human body is acceptable.
38B. Art representing the human body should be limited or forbidden.

39A. It is acceptable to force conversion by threats and intimidation.
39B. It is unacceptable to force conversion.

40A. My diet is strongly influenced by my religion.
40B. Religion is not relevant to my diet.

41A. My religion emphasizes the value of broad education.
41B. My religion does not emphasize the value of broad education.

42A. I value prescribed procedures for prayers, fasting, and holy days.
42B. I wish to be free of such prescribed procedures.

43A. My religion wants no birth control and unrestricted numbers of children.
43B. My religion values birth control and population management.

44A. Same gender partners are accepted fully and openly in my faith.
44B. Same gender partners are discouraged or forbidden in my faith.

45A. Rational thinking is encouraged.
45B. Rational thinking is discouraged.

46A. Suffering is punishment from a deity.
46B. Suffering has no relationship to punishment from an external source.

47A. Public schools are preferable.
47B. Religious controlled schools are preferable.

48A. I value epiphanies of extraordinary insight and changes of perspectives.

48B. I seek no such experiences.

49A. I am happy with my worldview just as it is.

49B. I am always searching, trying to change and develop my worldview.

50A. Discussion of religions can be productive and profitable.

50B. Discussion of religions is of little or no benefit.

Responses

We had been using the Religious Subsystem Preference Inventory in one of my university communication courses as an example of a kind of discussion facilitator. A student, a possible bride-to-be, remained after class. She explained that she and her fiancé came from families of very different religious backgrounds, describing some of the antagonisms between the two groups. She said, "We want to get married, but our families and friends don't want us to, and we're even beginning to wonder if it could work, ourselves." She planned to share the Inventory with her fiancé and with their extended families to see if that could help.

A month later, she updated me. They reviewed the items and shared their responses, including ever widening circles of family and friends in the process. Increasingly, they all could ask each other questions for further understanding, avoiding criticism. Two months later, their wedding invitation arrived in the mail.

•

An interfaith group asked me to facilitate dialogue among them. I divided them into small discussion circles and asked them to read aloud the inventory items, pausing after each to explain their perspectives as clearly as they could. This resulted, they later evaluated, in focusing them away from institutional issues and helped them to concentrate on each other as individuals, so that they talked about their preferences as human beings rather than as organizational members. They said this cut across denominational lines and helped them become a community of seekers.

•

Another group wanted to build its own hypothetical religious organization. Rather than discussing inherited institutions, they wanted to start from the creative end. Using the inventory as a discussion guide, they referred to their resulting collective options as a wish list for a spiritual home.

•

The self-defined *non-religious prodigal* described his disillusionment with organized religion encounters in the past and considered himself outside of religion. After taking a copy of the inventory home with him, he returned to say that he could specify clearly his preferences on every item and give the reasons why. For him, the experience precipitated a new definition of *religious* as including himself and everyone else, with varied preferences.

•

A message came from a participant at the conference where the Inventory was first presented. The minister said he had feared the worst at the convention, that it would break down into factions and debates, rather than finding points of similarity. Some of his personal anxieties had been realized when a group of audience members in one session physically attacked a speaker of a rival group. When the committee to draft a common charter, on which all religious communities needed to agree, could not come to consensus on the use of the word *God*, they left it out.

He felt that a tool like the inventory had universal application, by focusing on differences of views as perspective preferences rather than absolutes that remained mutually exclusive.

The Religion That Has No Name

As my quest continued, four interrelated aspects of spiritual perspective, of religion, became meaningful for me. They might be referred to as the religion that has no name, the religion of maps, the religion of process, and the religion of behavior.

The religion that has no name, nor ever can, is reality in all its aspects. Things as they are. Existence. What is happening. Wave the hands in both directions, indicating everything—that. *That* is the one real religion. It is right, true, whole, complete. It has no alternatives, no competitors. It is what is.

We have just gone beyond words. There can be no arguments here. There are no partial truths. We are pointing at the one great, omnipresent whole, everything, forces and elements as they actually exist. If there are spirits, protons, fission, novas— whatever and all—they simply exist. Or they don't. If they do, they may be named or unnamed. With or without our awareness that they exist. Changing, altering, gravitating, shifting, moving, revolving. Doing whatever they do, in whatever way they do it. If they do not exist, no amount of naming and pointing will call them into being.

•

Before an astronomer created the concept of galaxies beyond our own, the milky way concept prevailed, stars that looked liked spilled milk across the sky. In 1924, Edwin Hubble said the word *galaxies*. Plural. He applied the word to the multiple swirling masses of suns and gasses. But his voicing of that concept did not create the magnificent spirals and glowing pinwheels measured in light years, grouped in clusters and super clusters. Those were there already. They were the reality. The discoveries came later. The words came later. The words entered into the conceptualization of Hubble's verbal map, and then into dozens of verbal maps of other astronomers, and then into the general human awareness. Should every human with these concepts cease to be, the galaxies would continue to be what they are.

•

Whatever more there is, in the spread and grouping of energy and matter, across eons of light years, is there now, whether or not human awareness makes maps of them with words. This reality is one, single, functioning. There is no multiplicity of *what is*. No either-or. No maybe this or that. The *reality* continues. Angels, phantasma, neurons, or protons, if they exist, with or without a name, made up of whatever substances, simply *are* or *are not*.

This is what words gesture toward. This is what human symbols point at. It does not matter whether those symbols come from what humans call religion, science, or pop culture. Whatever may gesture toward it, the *reality* is *what exists*. If it does not exist, then no amount of gesturing will make it so.

The Religion of Maps

Second, we may consider religion as verbal maps. All of us map the *reality*, our limited impression of it, using symbols. Yet the symbol is not the same as the thing it represents, or purports to represent.

Now we enter the phase of words, charts, diagrams, mathematical formulas. These are symbols. These are used to make our symbolic maps. We make verbal maps every time we speak or write. Mapmakers, all of us. And all of our ancestors who could speak and make symbols. Mapping the pieces and parts of the *universal everything* as they experienced it and as they interpreted their experiences of it.

Some of these maps have names. People's names who made them. Groups' names who augmented them. The worldviews that organized and sought to perpetuate themselves as social structures, became the historical religions and philosophies, cults, sects, denominations, and movements.

Often their claims were mutually exclusive. The claims of many were such that if one was right, others had to be wrong. If one was best, the others were inferior. War, aggravation, competition could exist at this level, the level of mapmaking.

•

This is the realm of multiplicity. This is the realm where everyone's map is different from everyone else's. This is the level in which we use comparisons, analogies, similes, and metaphors.

We say this thing is like another thing in particular ways. Tribes that live in mountainous areas use analogies with mountain terms. Tribes that live in deserts use analogies of deserts.

English has a vocabulary of some half million dictionary words to use for mapping. Plus at least another five hundred thousand words of technical, deep-field specializations that do more detailed mapping. Plus the language of math in all its forms with which to do another kind of fine-tuning cartography. Plus several thousand languages and dialects other than English.

•

One's map is his or her worldview, philosophy, religion. One's unique rendering of his or her perception of reality. From all the stimuli that have reached us, from all of our reasoning and intuitive processing, our maps become the result. Our concept of gods and afterlives, of wealth, of human relationships, of the stars and space, of pizza and cherubim and snails, all are part of our maps. Some of the jottings on our maps may accord very closely with the first level reality and many aspects may not. Many aspects may be absent. Unnoticed. Undiscovered. Rejected. Beyond the telescopes and microscopes of our perceptions.

•

I rode a night train in Russia from St. Petersburg to Moscow. The compartments were jammed with people. In the after-midnight hours, many travelers climbed from their berths to stand in the corridor by the open windows breathing the rush of hot air, watching the shadowscape outside. What was the name of the city we had departed from? St. Petersburg, then Leningrad, then St. Petersburg again, what will it be named next? Whatever the ruling mapmakers impose on it. And why were the names of *Peter* or *Lenin* chosen? And by whom?

I climbed Ayers Rock that rises red and rounded in the middle of the Australian outback. But who was Ayers? And what was it called before Europeans arrived? *Uluru* to the Pitjatjantjara and

Yankunytjatara tribes. With a cave called *Mala Puta*, the pouch of the marsupial wallaby. In 1873 a European government surveyor saw the huge monolith and imposed on it the name of the governor of South Australia, Sir Henry Ayers. So did I stand on the top of *Uluru* or *Ayers Rock*? Or did I stand on a nameless stone reality which others had stamped with words from their differing verbal maps?

When I explored the bazaars of the Turkish city, was it *Istanbul*? Or did echoes of the name of the Roman emperor still make it *Constantinople*? What was it called before that? Whose map are we walking on?

I talked with people in a city in China, but was it *Beijing* or *Peking*? The schedule board at the airport gate in Tokyo had specifically spelled the destination as *Peking*. Yet when the plane landed, we were welcomed to *Beijing*. A difference in the regional dialects between those formerly and later in authority, a resident shrugged.

•

Wolves spray territory with their liquid scents, marking their range. Humans spray boundaries with names from their maps. Constantinople, Istanbul, Ayers Rock, Uluru, St. Petersburg, Leningrad. Every name imposed on every city, state, territory, tree, rock, mountain, or body of water came from someone's map. So did the name for every custom, creature, ceremony, or status, whether real or imagined, within every worldview. Organizations spattered about the words for angels and demons, seers and saints, communion and bar mitzvah, valhalla and hades and alcheringa, sin and redemption, resurrection and reincarnation. Claiming the reality as their own. Until the next wave came and sprayed the same reality, as they perceived it, with their new terms, reinterpreting it for themselves.

•

This is the level of theology. The nature of the deity according to our maps. The reality does not change, but our maps do. Age by age, and person by person. This is the realm of potential conflict, where our maps differ. Individuals and groups holding up their maps may find these differences and engage in conflicts over them. This is the level of the multiple of Christian denominations, of the vast numbers of variations of Islam, Judaism, Hinduism, Buddhism, the proliferation of sects, cults, and new movements. This is the realm of *my map is better than your map*. This is the arena in which battalions can hurl themselves at each other, with the victors holding their map high, proclaiming it as the *truth*.

•

This is the level of symbols, of words, of strokes of the pen, computer screens, readings of dials and electronic displays. This is the realm of every book ever written, every scroll inscribed, every sign posted, every word uttered to vibrate the air with its sound, every play produced, every film and video and television program, every piece of three-dimensional art, every painting, every musical composition. All of these demonstrate the use of symbols in order to map limited perceptions of reality. These are gestures, however complex, toward aspects of the ultimate reality or toward the non-existent renderings of our imagination. In the realm of maps, similarities and differences abound.

The Religion of Process

Third, we may also refer to religion as the *process* by which maps are made. The process of making verbal maps differs from the resulting maps, themselves. The grossness or refinement of these processes constitute a form or level of religion, the procedures by which symbols are handled, the importance given to them, the way they are drawn, inscribed, and interpreted.

•

There are ways of processing information that help us to make our maps as carefully as possible, and there are ways that have inherent problems. Some methods create dissension, while others foster harmony. We name processes: rational thinking, rhetoric, syllogisms, scientific method, research, documentation, intuition, statistical analysis, meditation, contemplation, mind focus, impulse, problem-solving sequences.

Two people observe the same event. Both interpret it differently. If they realize that they *interpret*, and how *interpretation* differs from *observation*, they may avoid dissension, and show respect for each other's inferences. They can learn to explain to each other how they came by those interpretations.

•

The standards of this level relate to how closely the processes we use help us to produce maps that are accurate. This is the realm of propaganda devices and of protection from their abuse.

Does one person have what he calls a *revelation* and expect others to accept it, whole and complete? What if another individual claims a separate private *revelation* and expects all others to accept it whole and complete? Are the two not potentially on a collision course? So standards are needed by which to judge the appropriateness of each personal map and the means by which it came into being. If we all do not have the potential to check the accuracy of claimed revelations and interpretations for ourselves, what validity can be attributed to them?

Here the use of metaphor, statistics, poetry, equations, descriptive prose, hypotheses, theorems, axioms, all are processes of mapping reality. When any speaker verbalizes a portion of his or her map, however simple the opinion expressed, it is transmitted through the process of symbol use. When the voices from behind the podiums or from the mountain tops speak, the listeners have means of evaluating the validity of the verbal product. Recognizing and analyzing *process* protects the listeners from the barrage of exploitation from demagogues, unscrupulous advertisers, would-be messiahs-for-profit, dictators, and all who would manipulate others by manipulating the symbols and maps.

The process of worldview mapmaking becomes the literacy of living.

The Religion of Behavior

Fourth, religion may also be regarded as *behavior*. Behavior occurs at every moment for all of us, in our actions and reactions to the myriad stimuli from other people, the elements, the extended environment.

Behavior demonstrates in the world what our internal map suggests is *reality*. The persons who pet dogs, or eat dogs, or leash dogs, or hunt with dogs, who have dogs for surrogate children, or breed new forms of dogs, or fight with dogs, or race them and bet on them, or have them pull sleds, or are guided by them, are all exhibiting the place dogs hold in their personal schemes of things on different maps. Their behavior externalizes their inner map.

Maps are internal. Behaviors are external.

•

Here, in the external behavior, we have the religion of deeds. How do people treat the environment? How many children do they contribute to the population? Do they own land or see land as open for everyone? Do they help sustain our ecosystem?

Centering in this realm, lies the behavior toward fellow humans. How are other humans labeled, and how are they reacted to? Are people treated as collections of Gypsies, albinos, bisexuals, wealthy, scrawny, aged, northern, fish-eating? Do we react to categories or to individuals? If reacted to by category, how does the behavior accorded other categories differ from the behavior toward the people in one's own? What of class, caste, race, economic status, age, sexual orientation, occupation? Does changing the label change the behavioral reactions?

Through history, this is the level that has pulled from two opposite directions. On the one side, behavior toward all as individuals, to be treated like oneself. On the other side, the hierarchying by categories that permits condescension, discrimination, segregation, genocide. Here is the level of *red, yellow, black and white, all are precious in his sight, Jesus loves the little children of the world.* And here is the level of the interpretation of Bible tales of Cain and Ham that turn them into a skin color and race and permit enslavement and violence in the name of a deity. Here is *do unto others as you would have others do unto you.* Here is Paul saying *slaves obey your master.* Do we see unique individuals rather than categories that can be marginalized and disposed of?

•

We see our maps exposing themselves in our behavior. When I served as a PTA president at a public school, another PTA president told me how, at her church, its leaders systematically met with new members moving into the city, to dissuade them from sending their children to public schools, telling them horrendous tales of violence and incompetence, and urging them, for the sake of their children's safety and souls, to send them to their private denominational schools. The official felt it was all based on smoldering racial prejudices and attempts to use the religious schools as a means of perpetuating segregation.

While I served as board president for the Montessori school, board members felt that current student diversity was insufficient, not educationally sound to have a student population that did not reflect the diversity of the general population. They proposed major fundraising projects for scholarships to be given to minority students, for the ultimate benefit of all the students.

At the time I volunteered to supervise a scout group, when I said I would not accept unless it could be racially integrated, an official expressed his opposition, saying it would be impossible, that parents would not agree to it, an attitude not validated by the resulting integrated group.

•

Of what value are the religious scriptures, scrolls, tapestries, regalia, houses of worship, chanting, rituals, meditation, prayers, fasting, slogans, proselytizing, missionaries, donations, and sermons, if they do not produce useful reactions of individuals to individuals? Do they produce the recognition that others need the same respect and justice as we would want? Does the treatment of other people as we would be treated carry over into the workplace, the government, the home, and the school? Beyond that, what of the behavior toward the other species of life, the environment, and the planet?

Potpourri

On my quest, I saw people's behavior externalizing their maps of their version of the ultimate reality, that were created through their various map-making processes. As the journey continued, I heard more of their stories.

•

I entered the dwelling in Africa. The Zulu owner welcomed us into his abode. "It is round, as you see," he explained, "not merely an architectural device. Since evil lurks in corners, this provides no place where it can lurk. So one builds a house without corners that is evil-free."

•

A man of Zoroastrian heritage said his father had been a keeper of the never-ceasing flame in the temple, staying locked in alone all night to tend the eternal fires. His father had told him that when everyone else left and the doors were fastened, he would sleep and let the fire die, rekindling it on the morrow before unlatching the doors. That the flame be kept alive was not important to him, only that the people believed it so.

•

In small boats in India, floating the predawn Ganges, whispers of wind and hushed voices welcomed the day with prayers. Into this tranquil atmosphere roared a motorboat, bouncing us all in its wake, its occupants shouting a Christian hymn. "American fundamentalists," mumbled one person in my boat. The Hindu at the helm smiled. "Look at them more closely when they pass again." The hymn-shouters circled, waving Bibles. "Japanese?" questioned another boater, disbelievingly. "Yes," smiled our oarsman. "Conservative fundamentalist Christians from Japan, of Shinto background, aggressively spreading their concepts to Hindus in India." "At least," said another, "it has an ecumenical flavor."

•

They all seemed to have but one arm functioning, the other being behind them. Faculty from the prestigious denominational college filled the sofa-rich reception chamber. They had flown me in for a conference, my greeter at the airport driving me to this reception. As we came in the door I witnessed this remarkable one-armed noiseless tableau. As my greeter introduced me, the gathering responded with a communal *welcome*, and noise returned, as did the arms, and hands holding alcoholic drinks. My host explained that their church forbids the imbibing of liquor and doing so can result in job loss. So with each new entry into the room, the arms once again disappeared, until the newcomer was identified as *safe*.

•

The youth's face, reflecting African ancestry, looked bemused by what he was about to say. He had heard that I had lived all my adult life in African-American neighborhoods, feeling that if everyone contributed diversity to where they lived, designations of neighborhoods by race could cease, and we could become neighborhoods of varied individuals.

He explained, "I was adopted as a child by a white family," describing how they had lived to the rural part of a western state bordering Canada. "There were no black people anywhere around," he said, and only after the family's recent move to Arkansas did he meet other African-Americans. "Some people expect me to know kinds of cultural things that I don't seem to, and are impatient with me." He grinned and asked if we could talk about *things*, and maybe I could help him ease into... He shrugged to complete the thought, adding, "It seems reasonable to me."

•

On the clear and sunny day, by a lake shore, the Dalai Lama spoke to the gathering of his views and how he respected the views of others. A listener near me shook her head up and down in affirmation, saying softly how much she appreciated hearing someone who was firm and clear in his own beliefs be so welcoming to diversity.

•

In a small parish, a family invited me to dine with them. The priest joined in, accompanied by the lady introduced as his secretary for more than thirty years, who went everywhere with him. After the priest and secretary had left, an out-of-towner referred to that *poor secretary working for so long in the same low-paying job.* A local explained. *We all know they've been a couple all these years, but no one makes an issue of it.*

•

I sat in a home in Australia, drinking tea as a family discussed their church activities. "It's such a lovely church," the hostess said, "quite a beautiful museum." She explained the museum-church: "It houses the relics of a past age when people believed in the superstitions of heaven and hell, and all the lovely old tales in the Bible. So it's like a museum of a precious part of our heritage. It's an important part of our lives. It's our socialization, our care-giving group, and our mutual support." Just as she knew of nobody who actively believed in Apollo or Athena anymore, but cherished the myths for their cultural value, so the Judeo-Christian traditions also afforded understanding of how our ancestors had developed. "It's a lovely museum-church and an important part of our lives," she said.

•

The gray-haired lady just inside a religious center handed me a program and pointed the way to the sanctuary. "Welcome," she said. Then, as if in explanation as to why she had spoken to me at all, she added, "I'm the greeter today so I have to speak to you. I'm not very good at it, and I wouldn't be so forward otherwise. If you want to know anything, ask someone else. We don't pressure." After the service, one member told me that there were some booklets I could read on a rack in another room that I could go find for myself. If I wanted. But not to feel pressured. "We're not unfriendly," a man rearranging the hymn books said. "First time I came, I thought they didn't want me here. Then I realized they leave people to themselves. Many other groups are like long infomercials. Here, they've gone the other way. I love it!"

•

I called the number in the phone book in Chicago, one of several listings for different congregations of the particular denomination I was exploring. I needed directions to their morning meeting. The lady's voice said, "No need to come this morning. We don't have anything special planned. You'd probably be bored. But it's up to you." I received similar responses after calling the other numbers and ended up having breakfast with a member of one of the congregations. She said, "We're all different in each group. People tend to gravitate toward whichever of our congregations makes them feel comfortable. Some dress up and some dress down. Some sing hymns and some don't sing at all. Many of us come from the rigid faiths and knew something was wrong somewhere. Some perfect person and his appointees are going to tell everyone else how to live? And blame this superiority on God? I don't think so! So we really appreciate each other and what we have now. This is truly a religious community."

•

The marathon runner described her decision to join a group that did not actively seek converts. "Everyone in my children's schools went to some church. When I said we didn't go anywhere, they looked like we had just broken out of Alcatraz. So we came to this place so the children could have a church name." She suddenly thought of something else. "Oh yes! The really important thing. The marketing strategies of some churches is to assume sin, and then they claim to own salvation. I couldn't raise my children that way, telling them that humans were evil. Here, the assumption is just the opposite. Children are good, filled with potential. We teach them to reason for themselves and to question authority. I tell mine to always ask me for explanations, and they need to ask the people in church the same thing and expect a decent explanation. An answer like *I'm your parent* is no better than *I'm your minister* or *I'm your prophet.*"

•

Speaking at a conference at Cambridge University afforded me the opportunity to talk with those interested in the ancient stone structures of the British Isles. One person described his daily journey to work that took him past Stonehenge as he tried to intuit the mind-set of its makers. He considered it a visible outer remnant of their inner worldview, in the same way that his auto, office, and home outwardly reflected his inner concepts. "And let anyone try to figure out those!"

•

Before the elections that would place Mandella in the presidency, I attended an international conference in South Africa. We conferred with individuals from the country's diverse backgrounds. Some voiced dire predictions of violence. An Afrikaner host said the townships, to which apartheid had segregated native Africans, were too volatile to consider home visits. But an individual living there took two of us by night, and he and his family welcomed us into their home. His elders told of their burdens under apartheid. The grandmother held my hand and said she had not thought to have one like me in her home to listen to her story. She told a rending account, reminiscent of all attempts to survive under oppression, in one of its many variations around the world. The next day the Afrikaner, having heard about the visit, voiced deep concern about what complications could have arisen.

•

The urgent voice on my office phone said, "You do diversity training, and we need help." She represented a major hospital complex. "Our operating room teams need your intervention." "As early as next month?" I asked, looking at the calendar. "No!" she said, "tomorrow!" Her surgery teams were made up of a variety of nationalities. Their antagonisms had surfaced and erupted, as they hurled epithets at each other from behind their surgical masks over their anesthetized patients on the operating table. They came from varied religious backgrounds, all of which had teachings of love, harmony, and unity, but now traded prejudicial insults. "Tomorrow!" she repeated, "Our ability to continue functioning is threatened."

•

Conducting a communication workshop for a nursing association, I asked for specific examples of communication problems for which they sought solutions. Foremost was the situation of a male doctor who refused to talk directly to male nurses. When faced with the need to convey information to them, even when they spoke to him directly, he would call a female nurse over, and in the presence of the male nurse, tell her what to do, then walk away without acknowledging his existence.

•

Along with university teaching, I conducted communication classes at a police academy, and also taught inmates in prison classes. Those at all three sites made candid observations about those at the other two locations. I wanted them to hear each others' viewpoints, conducted a study involving their assumptions about themselves and the other two groups, compiled the results, and shared them. Each group expressed surprise at how the others saw them, wondering how the others could have possibly made such unfounded projections.

•

During the first night of a communication course in prison, we had reviewed the coming activities, and I asked if there were any questions. One student-inmate raised his hand and asked, "Have you ever spoken to a captive audience before?" and the group erupted in laughter.

•

I asked a police officer dealing with gangs to come to campus to discuss communication within such groups. He first asked the class to identify the reasons why people join religious organizations. After they developed a list, he read the reasons he had received from gang members for joining their groups. The two lists were almost identical, and he asked the class to explain why.

•

The minister and I sat in after-dinner dialogue. He asked about my encounters with a variety of religious viewpoints. He started to express excited words about interrelationships between worldviews when he caught himself in mid-sentence and mid-gesture. The hand descended and the voice changed. "We must never talk of these things again," he said slowly. "If we go any further, I am on the verge of changing my views in ways that would interfere with my profession."

•

The Christian evangelist had gained national prominence. We conversed on a range of topics. In expressing opinions, I several times cited words of Jesus for mutual understanding. He looked quizzical. "Why do you keep quoting Jesus?" he asked, saying that Jesus' opinion was no more important than that of anyone else, that Jesus was no different than the rest of us. I had heard this minister's stirring sermons and pointed out that the attitude just expressed was not included in his pulpit presentations. He said, "No, they might disturb some of the congregations. Besides, Jesus' ideas won't do them any harm, and that's what they're paying to hear."

•

I stood in an Orthodox church in Athens, Greece. Some non-Greek visitors were surprised to find no seats in the sanctuary. The cleric explained that when one is concentrating on the divine, the body does not feel fatigue and seats are never provided, except for a few old and infirm.

At a Greek Orthodox church in America, I raised the question why permanent pews were installed in their sanctuary. The priest, originally from Greece, sighed and shrugged, saying, "These people don't understand spiritual concentration and have to be pampered. But they would stop coming if we removed the pews. It's a compromise I don't like. I don't know if I can ever get them to that level or not."

•

The Hindu visitor gazed at the vegetarian feast spread out before us by our hosts, who wanted to honor his religious practices. He said that although he had never eaten meat, he didn't know what a non-carnivorous diet had to do with religion. "I didn't eat meat because it was never served at home." He asked me to go with him for his first visit to a grocery store's meat section. He stood in shock at the sight of trays of various cuts and hurried toward the door. Outside, sweating and dizzy, he said he didn't know exactly how to explain what he was experiencing, but that it must be akin to what meat-eating persons might experience if they entered a place filled with packaged human parts.

•

The nuns sat behind corded curtains and spoke of their mission: to read of world troubles and do in-depth research on causes, and then to continually pray for solutions. They took a semi-vow of silence, to speak only of needful things, but to avoid frivolous patter. My students interviewed them through the curtains about their communication within the cloister of their self-imposed confinement, never leaving, except for illness or death, studying for years and decades.

Back in our university classroom, the students, who had studied world history themselves, expressed their shock at realizing that those nuns had a grasp of world affairs far exceeding their own and even that of their teachers. The students grappled with the frustration of that magnitude of study and insight locked away with the perpetual murmur of prayers inside those confined rooms, instead of being shared.

•

Denominational representatives asked me to serve as advisor to their national committee to encourage greater racial diversity among its congregations. Its members had marched, demonstrated, written letters, supported anti-segregatory laws, worked for fair housing, jobs, and services. But now, years since many of those overt activities of which they were proud, their gatherings were still largely non-diverse. At the initial meeting, a perplexed lady asked, "With all this activity for the idea of social change, how many of us personally socialize with people of backgrounds different from ourselves?" Three out of fifty raised their hands.

•

The religious organization called me to come across half a continent as consultant for a serious communication problem. Their increasingly frequent board meetings had grown to six hours in length, straining their schedules. I sat as a silent observer through one of the long, convoluted, inconclusive sessions. By the time of the following meeting, I had completed my internal communication audit, and intervened throughout, keeping the discussion on topic and the decision-making steps in focus. They completed everything in a half hour. They had evolved an internal culture that assumed that the more important matters were, the more time they required. Now, with all the tools at hand for short, effective task-oriented sessions, they displayed all the characteristics of people in culture-shock, displaced and anxious. In my followup, I found that they chose to revert to their former long and thus important meetings of sacrificial effort, but with few resulting activities.

•

The call came to my university office phone from an international corporation headquarters. Complaints had been made about one of their high ranking male officials making disparaging remarks about females. "We don't want to fire him," said the corporate executive, "but we want him to understand a new perspective and want to hire your services." He asked me to work with the official one on one, to help him orient to the concept of people as individuals, not by gender, not by categories.

When I hung up the phone, I mused that we were about to engage in a truly religious practice, that has the power, when implemented, to precipitate a paradigm shift in individuals and societies. When the official flew into town and walked into my office, he said, "Serious, isn't it." One of the most serious undertakings a human being can deal with.

•

In Italy, at the mountainside monastery built on the wooded slopes by Assisi where St. Francis had walked, I spoke with young priests training for their missions, from various parts of the world. A red-haired European spoke enthusiastically of the adventure on which he had embarked. An African youth focused on his aims when he received his first post. A young man from Asia cleaned the walkway while he mentioned the many forms, including sweeping, that service to God may take, though he hoped for something more significant in the future.

•

The city task force I served on worked for two years to prepare a proposal for the city board of directors that would suggest a way to deal with racial and cultural diversity on the individual and institutional levels for the twenty-first century. Several of us were appointed subsequently to the resulting Commission on Racial and Cultural Diversity. A city official came to one of our meetings to hear the recommendations. He heard, instead, a series of personal stories of deprivation of rights, of perceived unfairness. *But what are the policies you recommend,* the administrator kept asking, as the stories unfolded. One of the panel suggested that the roots of any policies came from these individual events that gave a name and a face to both discrimination and equality, and we had to hear the experiences first.

•

"Not all the civil rights martyrs died immediately," she said. Her close relative had been the first African-American to integrate a particular school, a solitary lodestone for collective hostility, one of a cadre of individuals who helped change the system by their presence as *the first.* Years later, this lady was recalling that past and its impact on the person who had recently chosen to end his own life. "What he went through," she said, "no one understood. He had received into himself the accumulated poison of so much hate, he finally had to lay the burden down the only way he knew how." She sighed, "And all the martyrs weren't black. That local white man who stood up for everyone's rights, look what they did to him." She recounted how his neighbors, church, and relatives boycotted his business until he went bankrupt, excluded him and his wife from their activities and harassed his children until they turned on their father for ruining their lives, and his wife left him. He moved from his hometown to survive, and the lady described how "he still wanders around, poor, never accepted by his people, a living

martyr for the stand he took." She wiped tears from her cheeks.
"They'll both get their rewards in heaven."

•

In Spain, I talked to a local historian about the country's
development. "One of the great impacts of our heritage," he said,
"came when the Christian-influenced government drove out the
Jews and the Moslems, since both groups had so enriched the
country before. They had choices of leaving, death, or
conversion."

•

Before entering the church sanctuary to speak, my introducer
told me that I would receive a generous offering from the
congregation. When I said that I wished the offering to be kept
for their outreach projects, he and the other platform participants
huddled, after which he explained that they were working to
develop generosity in their parishioners. To have offerings
returned by the speaker would be counterproductive and set a bad
precedent, as the congregation might begin to expect others to
do the same.

•

One of my university classes studying small group
communication pursued topics of their choice. One group chose
prostitution, contacting the city social worker responsible for
keeping records of those so involved. After their interview with
her in her office, she had volunteered any further assistance they
wished. They asked her to come to class on the day of the
discussion to help field questions, adding jokingly, bring a client.

She did. The smartly dressed lady, who could have stepped
from a fashion catalog, entered the classroom with the social
worker. After the group had provided a historic timeline of
prostitution in cultures around the world, they came to the
question period from the audience of other class members. They
introduced the social worker who in turn introduced her client.

The client complimented the group on its objective, well-researched account of her profession. To a question as to whether she had ever considered going to school and getting a degree for a *real profession*, she responded that she had her master's degree in business administration and had chosen this as a lucrative occupation, with a six figure salary and stock options in the corporation that employed her to serve their international clientele. She was surprised that the "educated" class members did not realize that major corporations had women and men of her profession on their payrolls.

A muscled male athlete, blushing and staring at the floor, stood and cleared his throat, saying he had recently come to know Jesus Christ as his personal savior, suggesting she do the same and give up this sinful way of life. She regarded him in puzzlement for a moment and then explained that she considered herself a saved Christian and staunch supporter of her church, as were her husband and children. She then added that if he had a Bible with him and could show her where her profession was not an acceptable one, she would never practice her activities again. He pulled a Bible from his case and began searching.

•

The aggressive denomination had opened what they called a *culture center* on one of the Pacific islands. To this profitable enterprise, they brought an array of newly converted natives from a variety of island cultures to perform traditional dances for the entertainment of paying tourists. I asked some of the native converts privately about the attraction of this religion when compared to their traditional perspectives. They looked around first, and then explained that among themselves they still practiced their *own way of life*, but that the denomination provided food, shelter, and wages, and all they had to do to gain these benefits was to say they believed.

•

Opening my email, I found the subject *rib* on the list. A *joke you might enjoy*, the sender said and forwarded this: At Sunday School, they were teaching how God created everything, including human beings. Johnny seemed especially intent when they told him how Eve was created out of one of Adam's ribs. Later in the week, his mother noticed him lying down and said, "What's the matter?" He responded, "I have a pain in my side. I think I'm going to have a wife."

•

I went for a general physical checkup. The physician suggested an overall full-torso X-ray to file just for future reference. We looked at the results. "Ever give you any trouble?" he asked, gesturing across the top third of the negative. "Where?" I asked, not knowing to what he referred. "The ribs." "The ribs? What about them?" "Your extra ribs." "Extra ribs?" "Yes. Didn't you know you have two extra ribs?" I thought of my childhood church and science class experience and laughed.

•

I stood on the Delphian hills in Greece with others circling the navel-stone, the *omphalos*, marking the focal-point of the world. Zeus' two golden eagles had winged their way from the two ends of the earth to arrive together at its very center. The stone marked the site. And where, we could speculate, lies the center of each of our worlds? Where is our personal *omphalos*?

Context

Building a worldview involves creating inferences to explain the observed, guessing at contexts to give explanation and meaning. I was looking for a simple daily-life example of an event about which the circumstances leading up to it were unknown, for which a context would be a matter of speculation. I found it unexpectedly in New Mexico.

Driving to an Albuquerque shopping area rimmed by stores, I parked. Across from me remained one empty parking space, marked *Handicapped*. In the space next to that one, a driver was getting out of his vehicle. At that moment, into the handicapped space drove a car without a handicapped tag. A gentleman of advancing age got out and started walking toward a store. The man from the adjacent car saw the tagless car and the man walking away, without wheelchair, crutch, or cane. The observer called, "Hey! You can't park there! That space is for the handicapped!" The walker turned, at a distance, starting to mouth something, but turned again and sputtered on his way.

After going to a store, when I returned to my car, the original shouter and his car were gone. In its place, another automobile had parked. A man sat in the driver's seat reading a newspaper, waiting for a companion who had gone to shop, having no idea of the previous episode.

I saw the person returning who had parked in the handicapped space. His gait was determined now, his face a mask of augmenting displeasure. He did not realize that the car and driver next to him had changed. He walked past his own auto, straight to the next one. With both fists, he pounded on the window and shouted at the driver, "When you're ninety years old, you *are* handicapped!" He then turned, got into his own car, and drove off. The other driver, with slack jaw, stared unblinking toward his car window where the apparition had appeared, pounding and shouting words without a context.

Our lives are filled with strange people and phenomena pounding on the windows of our awareness, making no immediate sense to us. We seek contextual stories to explain the mysteries of life.

•

I also found an example of life events impinging on us unexpectedly over which we have no control, where *we* are out of context. In New York City, I searched the labyrinthine conference center for the room of my next session, ending up on a level of totally deserted hallways and closed meeting rooms. Suddenly one of the doors burst open and people erupted, with the New York Governor heading the entourage and rushing straight in my direction. Double doors flung open on the other side of the hall, and the press corps spewed forth, microphones poised and cameras flashing and questions being shouted. I became the epicenter of the two waves of people, both of which moved so rapidly that they closed me in the middle of their constricting circle. I stood head to head with the Governor, with reporters pushing at my back, thrusting microphones around my shoulders and sides into our inches-apart faces.

Somewhere in the news world's archives, I imagine photos and videotapes of that moment existing, with the *unidentified person* in the middle of it all, pressed up against the Governor, totally out of context, for which neither the media nor the Governor's staff have any explanation.

•

"I died," the woman told me, an event that gave new context to her life. She explained that after going to the hospital for surgery, she expired on the operating table. She told of maintaining total awareness, her *perspective* rising above her body. Of the passage up and out, moving toward the light beyond, meeting a figure that exuded peace and non-judgment. He reviewed every moment of her life with her and described positive alternative behaviors. He explained that the purpose of each event was to discover the values such as truth, trust, honesty, patience, understanding, justice, mercy, gratitude, comfortable relationships, and happiness, and to develop them day by day with others. A choice, the figure said, to remain or to return. To stay in this place of tranquility was her personal choice, but to return, for the sake of family.

"I had been an atheist before the operation, unconnected to any religious organization," she said. When she reawakened, she felt that the practice of these virtues was the goal of life. She assumed that the purpose of truly religious organizations is to define and study these virtues and help each other put them into daily practice in all aspects of living. She planned to visit every religious organization within a two-hour driving distance of her home to discover which one most vigorously pursued this goal and to join. She promised to notify me of the result.

Months later, she said, "Not one was primarily emphasizing what my life-reviewer told me was the purpose of religion and of living, to the degree I needed," and joined none of them. Yet she had found individuals within the groups who understood that there seemed to be a universal spiritual core which everyone has the potential of discovering, developing, and applying. These became what she considered as her new community, in her new context.

•

I was asked to work with a children's group to help enlarge their awareness and practice of positive qualities. First I asked them to name negative characteristics. They flooded the room with words such as lazy, stupid, stubborn, angry, clumsy, hateful. When I asked them to role-play behavior associated with each word, they vividly complied.

Next I asked for terms denoting positive qualities. Silence filled the room, punctuated with a few hesitant offerings—good, nice, OK. When asked to demonstrate these, they became unmoving and rigid. Being good translated as doing nothing. The word *no* had been learned long before *yes*. When asked for descriptions of other people, they used terms such as those related to race, gender, and size.

We undertook a series of activities to introduce dozens of positive terms, accompanied with definitions and behavioral demonstrations, such as trust, truth, justice, mercy, kindness, compassion, thoughtfulness, enthusiasm, humor, inventiveness, love, sincerity, loyalty, friendliness. When anyone demonstrated such behaviors, we named and commended it, encouraging everyone to join in.

With repeated practice, the children increasingly described each other, not by race, gender, or size, but as a collection of positive attributes. When they could see these characteristics in others, they began to see and like the same qualities in themselves.

I also worked with an adult group, including some of the children's parents. They agreed to experiment with calling attention to the positive behaviors of the children and to exclude references to the negative ones. Instead of saying, *You are messy tracking in dirt*, they would observe the times when no dirt was tracked in, and comment at that time on the thoughtfulness and cleanliness. Soon the children were saying the same things to their siblings and parents as they noticed and named these positive traits. As the use of "yes" increased, the use of "no" became almost unnecessary.

Some parents reported their difficulty in reorienting old habits but described the change as pleasant for the whole family. The more everyone focused on positive characteristics, the more such behavior increased and the negative diminished. Disciplinary measures tended to become obsolete in the newer context. They used fewer physical descriptors for others and increasingly identified them by clusters of positive attributes.

A parent reported his initial concern when he received a call at home one night from his son's school teacher. She assured him that nothing was wrong, but that she had a question about his son that was difficult to say. She described how those in her class tended to cluster on the playground by ethnicity and gender, except for one, the son. He went from group to group, enjoying them all. "He doesn't seem to see groups," said the teacher, "but appears to enjoy individuals. He brings people together who otherwise wouldn't associate. And when he describes people, he never uses race or color or what they look like, but mentions the most remarkable qualities that make me appreciate and see the students in a new way. He even sees me in that way, and I'm feeling a self-esteem that's hard to describe." She paused and then said, "My question is, how did this happen? We're all benefiting without even realizing it."

The Ministry to Which We Are Called

I encountered worldviews by the tens, the hundreds, the thousands. The ministry to which we are all called is an awakening to being human. In differing stories, in varied voices, from diverse traditions, from philosophy to science, all are called, whatever the backgrounds, to be human, to seize our common connection with the elements of the nebulae and galaxies and each other.

With a body made of the elements of the earth, with blood nearly the consistency of sea water coursing in our veins, thinking with the neural-electric energy that pulses within us, a fragment of the forces that stretch across the cosmos, we have the common ancestor of stardust and electric charges. From the earth, air, fire, and water quadrants of ancestral lore, to DNA models of our biological heritage, we map our structures and our ideas. We give names to functions and feelings and set about to fine tune the theories.

Theories break and fall apart and meld into others. Paradigm shifts turn our lives about in a day and jangle societies with aftershocks of quaking re-perceptions. We create lists of procedures that become cannons, laws, moral codes, ethical prescriptions, and constitutions. We sing songs that articulate our pains and passions. We mix paints and shape marble and metals to symbolize our visions.

Lilies and lavender waft fragrances whatever the names superimposed on them. So the reality of existence beyond human comprehension courses on, by the names of any gods or galaxies applied, whatever the analogies and anthropomorphic transparencies overlaid upon it. The magic and myths of all cultures offer fragments hinting at possible paths toward rebirth into a new frame of thinking and relating that some of our ancestors have encountered along their ways. We need not waste our time throwing stones and missiles at each other's metaphors while the existence awaits our exploration. The adventure surrounds us, pervades us, *is* us and all things beyond.

We can let the similes abound and the theorems multiply. The quest is on, by day and night, waking and dreaming, to plot our ways and share the findings, in novels and newscasts, in treatises and sermons. We can speculate, reason, conclude, experiment, and infer. We can do them all well, with energy and caution, respecting the wholeness of the web of existence.

We encounter paradoxes and oxymorons and find personality preferences contrary to expectations. Sifting the bogus from the genuine, the huckster from the helpful, the sycophant from the sincere—the task is at hand, always, everywhere.

The ministry to which we are called includes service to each other, wherever we are and in whatever manner is available. Foremost is the certainty that we are of *one blood* and of multiple unique capabilities. The recognition of our fellow humans as equals remains the first grace and foremost bounty we can bestow.

We are one, thee and I, comes out in a thousand ways of looking, greeting, listening, beholding our common beatitudes and sufferings with fondness and simplicity. This realization erodes the non-existent dualisms and categorizations we invent and pretend are real justifications for domination.

We can become mapmakers *extraordinaire*, always perfecting our art and science of crafting symbols to make maps reflecting our progressive consciousness of reality. We can hone our ability to identify the willfully misleading maps of others. We can protect our children against those inaccurate renderings by helping our heirs to become mapmakers *extraordinaire* in their own right.

All people have a worldview in a quartet of levels: reality, map, mapping process, and behavior. Every named religion can be evaluated by how it regards the wordless reality, the map it supports, the process of map-making it teaches, and the behavior exhibited by its institutions and members. These four aspects cut across all worldviews, named or unnamed. The process of mapping can be learned and its effectiveness continually improved. As a result, the maps that guide our lives can be constantly upgraded by adding positive factors and replacing the faulty.

A kind of biological and mystical anthem sounds to a common heartbeat of humanity. A chorus, repeating our mutual invitation. The ministry to which we are called is the ministry of service to each other and of sustaining the richness of our planetary environment, wherever we are and in whatever manner is available. Our stories are parts of one story.

> the arch of incandescence hovers above
> moving with the discoverers
> shifting its colors
> transmuting in mists of mutating hues
> tinges yet unnamed
> in shades outside known wavelengths

the explorers transfiguring
perpetually becoming and extending

up to the surface
up to the mountains
out to the planets
out to the stars
out to all that is
and that we can become
beyond the visible spectrum

•

Beyond the Visible Spectrum A memoir of episodes from the author's research of worldviews around the globe, in Africa, Asia, Europe, South and North America. Human behavior is the outer visible result of our inner worldviews, which are *beyond the visible spectrum*.

Postmodern Zen: Paradox & Process Zen is perhaps the most used word in the world to describe the human ability for a sudden insight, while postmodern implies a transition from unexamined assumptions, a fresh start. The book looks at the hybrid vigor of these combined perspectives, and explores core questions common to us all.

LUCIAN, a novel Graduating from college, he fell through the sound bites, slogans, and social roles surrounding him. Retreating to the desert, he encountered others, such as the once-dead code talker, the cliff-dwelling tribe of one, a zebra-riding population-clock watcher. His odyssey reflects all of our paths of discovery. What if life kept happening while you made other plans? What if you were Lucian?

TRICKSTER, a novel The mythic trickster figures appear in stories from cultures around the world. A museum director who studies them from long ago and far away suddenly encounters one here and now, with an invitation to an unusual writing class that begins to re-write his own life in unexpected ways.

For information on presentations for Book Clubs and other groups, contact Allan Ward at 501-664-5921 or alward@ualr.edu.